But Wh́o Do *You* Say I Am?

Bishop John A. Marshall

With an introduction by,
James Cardinal Hickey

Ambassador Books
Worcester, Massachusetts

Published with ecclesiastical approbation.

Grateful acknowledgement is made to the Augustinians of the Assumption for permission to use the 19th Century icon, Christ Pantocrator for the cover of this book. The icon is on display in the Icon Exhibit at St. Anne's Shrine in Fiskdale (Sturbridge), Massachusetts.

ISBN: 0-9646439-0-1
Library of Congress Catalog Card Number: 99-069331

Published in the United States by Ambassador Books, Inc.
71 Elm Street, Worcester, Massachusetts 01609
(800) 577-0909

Printed in Canada.

For current information about all titles from Ambassador Books,
visit our website at:
www.ambassadorbooks.com

TABLE OF CONTENTS

Foreword

JAMES CARDINAL HICKEY

I AM HONORED TO OFFER AN INTRODUCTORY WORD TO THESE reflections by Bishop John Marshall. I knew him not only as a brother bishop and colleague, but above all as a friend. Perhaps the best way I can introduce you to his book is to introduce you to my friendship with him.

The year was 1969. I was the newly appointed Rector of the Pontifical North American College—our U.S. seminary in Rome. It was a time of upheaval, even turmoil, in many institutions. Unfortunately, seminaries were no exception to that trend. I knew I needed wise, level-headed and holy co-workers. That's just what I found in the then Father John Marshall.

He was serving the seminary as spiritual director. As I listened to him speak of his work, I knew how much he loved it. I knew he was providing sound formation for our future priests. I sensed that he was more than competent; he was bedrock solid in his love for the Lord, for the Church, and for the priesthood.

But among my many problems as seminary Rector were severe financial problems. I desperately needed help in the financial management of the College. All attempts to find that help had failed. Tucked away in the recesses of my memory, however, was an awareness that the future

Bishop Marshall was indeed a very good financial manager. So I asked him to make a difficult sacrifice: to begin serving as "economo," or business manager, of the College. I will never forget his response. He paused, prayed for a moment, and then told me he would do whatever the Church needed him to do. With that, our growing friendship was sealed.

Father Marshall proved to be a very good business manager. But he was first and foremost a priest. He earned the deep respect of both faculty and students. He was a rock upon whom I relied for all kinds of advice.

During my tenure as Rector, Father Marshall was appointed the Bishop of Burlington, Vermont. I was sorry to see him leave the College, but happy that the Church had entrusted him with greater responsibilities. In the mid-1980s, Bishop Marshall was tapped again, this time to conduct a study of all U.S. seminaries, a study requested by the Holy See. He fulfilled that challenging task with the same steady sense of responsibility, fairness, and courage that I had witnessed years before when we worked together at the North American College.

In 1989, he was appointed Bishop of Springfield, Massachusetts, a further recognition of his talents and generous service. I was present for his installation and rejoiced with him. But soon word came that my good friend was suffering from bone cancer. My rock solid friend was facing a devastating, incredibly painful disease. Bishop Marshall faced it as he had every other challenge in his life: with faith, courage, integrity, and love. He surrendered his life and his priesthood to Jesus.

In doing so, he knew the answer to the question, "Who do you say I am?" He knew Jesus, Son of God and Son of Mary. He knew Jesus the Priest. He knew Jesus as Brother, Savior and Son of God.

I invite you now to read and ponder Bishop Marshall's reflections on the Lord Jesus. Let him challenge you in his quiet, persistent way—the way he challenged all of us who knew and loved him. Let him help you answer Jesus' question: "But Who Do You Say I Am?"

A Note on the Text

AT THE TIME OF HIS DEATH, BISHOP MARSHALL LEFT SEVERAL volumes of writings on the Gospels. We have no way of knowing whether the bishop considered publishing these writings or intended to use them for his own personal reflections or perhaps as a source for future homilies.

But upon examining these writings, it was quickly evident that they contained a deep understanding of God's Word and a practical but profound perspective on the Christian life. Sharing them in the form of a book seemed a logical and natural consequence.

Especially intriguing was the text for the present volume. In it, Bishop Marshall examines each question asked in the Gospels. His approach seems in some respects to make the Gospel more personal to the individual reader. When Jesus asks a question, it is we, the readers, who must answer it. And when others ask Jesus questions, we have a more immediate understanding of the obstacles and the enmity that he faced.

Each Gospel has a power and beauty all its own. And the more time we spend with a Gospel, the more we appreciate this fact. Truly, to plumb the depths of the Gospels, we must examine them from every possible perspective and in every possible light. That is one of the things Bishop Marshall was apparently doing when he studied the Gospels in the light of the questions Jesus asked and then in the light of the questions asked by others. Throughout his study, Bishop Marshall keeps the focus right where it belongs—on Jesus and his teaching.

Jesus uses questions to provoke a person to deeper thought, or to help a person arrive at the truth. If the listener accepts Jesus' challenge, he/she goes deeper. On the other hand, if the listener refuses the challenges, he/she walks away into obscurity.

The Bishop's reflections can be looked upon as his own musings, brief jottings for further meditation, or thoughts to be developed in future homilies. Our task as his readers is to take his thoughts as a foundation and to build our meditations upon them.

The question used for the title of this book, "But Who Do You Say I Am?" is a primary question. In one way or another, Jesus is quoted as posing this question directly to his disciples in three of the four Gospels (Matthew 16:15, Mark 8:29, Luke 9:20). And the Gospel of John recounts a similar incident where Peter affirms the truth of who Jesus is.

As a reflection on Luke 24:30-32, Bishop Marshall says, "We should try to set souls on fire, not by short-lived emotion, but with the long-burning flame of Truth." This statement may well describe the direction of his life and teaching.

— *Sister Ann Marie Marshall, RSM*

PART ONE

*Questions Jesus
Asked in the Gospels*

Questions are a very important part of Jesus' ministry. Like many good teachers, he uses them to instruct and to focus attention on a subject. But he does more than that. Jesus' questions address the individual listener. They are not general or theoretical questions. They are personal and particular. For example, in the first question in Matthew, Jesus does not ask, "If people love those who love them, what good will it do them?" Instead he asks, "If *you* love (only) those who love *you*, what recompense will *you* have?" The effect is that Jesus asks his questions of each of us in a personal and particular way. He is not merely talking to the person standing next to us, he is speaking to each of us, to me and to you.

The reason, of course, is that Salvation is an individual thing. It is practical and not theoretical. It is something that happens to each individual or it does not.

In this book, Bishop Marshall, has explored every question asked in the Gospels. In Part One, they are the questions that Jesus asked. In Part Two, they are the questions others asked.

In composing this work, Bishop Marshall imitates Jesus because he asks us to take the questions personally, to receive them into our consciousness, to reflect on them and, in a sense, to digest them.

But Bishop Marshall does not stop there. He draws lessons from the questions and invites us to put the answers into action. After all, Christianity is an active way of life; we receive grace so that we may act upon it.

In short, this is a practical book, not a theoretical book. By using it, we are continually challenged to grow by applying the Gospel to our lives.

For many of us, meditation seems mysterious and difficult. When using the Meditations sections of the book, our meditations should be very practical. First, we should seek to understand the question that Jesus is asking us. A specific question may seem quite simple, but if we examine it, it will probably turn out to be quite profound. We shall also see that the answer to a question calls for a specific response on our part.

For example, if we meditate on the question, "Who do you say I am?" we will respond with Peter, "You are the Messiah, the Son of the Living God." And as we meditate, the immense implications of that statement will begin to occur to us. Jesus is God's Son, who was born into the world. He is our Savior who comes to change our lives and free us from darkness. If we hear him and follow him, he is our doorway to eternal life. In this meditation we hear the good news, that Jesus is Lord. The lesson that we draw from it is that we must follow him by living the Gospel.

It is a life-changing lesson.

CHAPTER ONE

Questions Jesus Asked in the Gospel of Matthew

Matthew 5:46-48

"For if you love those who love you, what recompense will you have? Do not the tax collectors do the same? And if you greet your brothers only, what is unusual about that? Do not the pagans do the same? So be perfect, just as your heavenly Father is perfect."

MEDITATIONS & LESSONS

+ We are called to nothing less than perfection. Perfection is the ideal we should aim for in our daily lives and in the way we treat others.
+ Our attitude should be ecumenical. We should reach out not only to people of our own faith or ethnic or economic background, but to people of different races and religions, too.

✦　Our charity must extend to strangers and to the unlovable—the homeless, the mentally ill, the outcasts. If we extend our charity to only our brothers and sisters, then there is nothing unusual about our love.

✦　Tax collectors were almost universally disliked. So if we are like tax collectors, and limit our love to only those who love us, then our love is small indeed.

MATTHEW 6:25-33

"Therefore I tell you, do not worry about your life, what you will eat [or drink], or about your body, what you will wear. Is not life more than food and the body more than clothing? Look at the birds in the sky; they do not sow or reap, they gather nothing into barns, yet your heavenly Father feeds them. Are not you more important then they? Can any of you by worrying add a single moment to your life-span? Why are you anxious about clothes? Learn from the way the wild flowers grow. They do not work or spin. But I tell you that not even Solomon in all his splendor was clothed like one of them. If God so clothes the grass of the field, which grows today and is thrown into the oven tomorrow, will he not much more provide for you, O you of little faith? So do not worry and say, 'What are we to eat?' or 'What are we to drink?' or 'What are we to wear?' All these things the pagans seek. Your heavenly Father knows that you need them all. But seek first the kingdom of God and his righteousness, and all these things will be given you besides."

MEDITATIONS & LESSONS

✦　We can spend a lot of time being concerned about our external condition—how we appear to others—rather than our internal, spiritual condition. But clothing and external appearances are relatively unimportant. They are the concerns of pagans, and we can get along without them. Our spiritual condition is much more important.

✦   Worry never helped anyone—God is taking care of us.

✦   Good use of one's life is more important than sustaining it for a longer time or simply maintaining a more healthy condition.

MATTHEW 7:1-4

"Stop judging, that you may not be judged. For as you judge, so will you be judged, and the measure with which you measure will be measured out to you. Why do you notice the splinter in your brother's eye, but do not perceive the wooden beam in your own eye? How can you say to your brother, 'Let me remove that splinter from your eye,' while the wooden beam is in your eye?"

MEDITATIONS & LESSONS:

✦   Mind your own business first. We should not concentrate on the faults of others while we are blind to our own faults.

✦   If we expect God to be merciful in his judgment of us, we must be merciful in our judgments of others.

✦   It is the greatest hypocrisy to notice other's faults while overlooking our own.

MATTHEW 7:9-10

"Which one of you would hand his son a stone when he asks for a loaf of bread, or a snake when he asks for a fish?"

Meditations & Lessons

✦   God is our Father; he loves us and will help us. He is infinitely more kind and loving than our earthly parents, and we can expect him to act that way.

✦   We should remember that Jesus told us to ask, and said that if we did so we would receive. The Father's willingness to respond to our requests shows us how much he loves us and is concerned about us.

✦   Do unto others as you would have them do unto you.

Matthew 7:16:

"Do people pick grapes from thornbushes, or figs from thistles?"

Meditations & Lessons

✦   Good begets good, evil begets evil. Good people perform good deeds, and evil people perform evil actions.

✦   By their fruits you will know them. We can tell whether or not someone is good by the quality of his or her actions.

✦   If there is evil or sin in one's life, even though it is hidden, that sin will manifest itself through some action.

✦   Think of the truly virtuous people you know; they may not be conspicuous, in fact, they may be unknown to most people. But they do exist, and they exert great influence on those who know them.

Matthew 7:21-23

"Not everyone who says to me, 'Lord, Lord,' will enter the kingdom of heaven, but only the one who does the will of my Father

in heaven. Many will say to me on that day, 'Lord, Lord, did we not prophesy in your name? Did we not drive out demons in your name? Did we not do mighty deeds in your name?' Then I will declare to them solemnly, 'I never knew you. Depart from me, you evildoers.' "

MEDITATIONS & LESSONS

✦ These spectacular deeds are not necessarily the works that God looks for in his followers. These are great works in the eyes of men, but not necessarily in the eyes of God.

✦ When we look for credit, we drain our works of their goodness and receive an earthly reward—the gratification of having others think well of us—rather than the gratification of an eternal reward.

✦ Every good work is much more to the credit of God's grace rather than to our efforts.

MATTHEW 8:26

"Why are you terrified, O you of little faith?"

MEDITATIONS & LESSONS

✦ The question contains the answer; the terrified have little faith.

✦ The miracles of the Gospel were meant to strengthen our faith as well as the faith of the Apostles.

✦ If we are convinced of God's love, no earthy calamity should cause fear and panic.

✦ Fear never produces any positive results.

Matthew 9:3-4

Some of the scribes said to themselves, "This man is blaspheming." Jesus knew what they were thinking, and said, "Why do you harbor evil thoughts?"

Meditations & Lessons

+ Sins of thought are as great or even greater than those of action because they tarnish one's whole attitude.

+ Our minds are more often focused on worldly things than upon God.

+ As human beings, we seem to have a natural propensity to compare ourselves to others, often times discounting their efforts or imputing poor motives on their actions. This is a tendency we should resist.

+ Goodness is more powerful than evil, compliments are more effective than criticism.

Matthew 9:15

"Can the wedding guests mourn as long as the bridegroom is with them? The days will come when the bridegroom is taken away from them, and then they will fast."

Meditations & Lessons

+ If we are in the presence of Christ, we cannot be mournful. We must be joyous, no matter what the situation.

+ If we have a spirit of joy in Christ, it will be contagious and will lead others to him.

MATTHEW 9:28

When he entered the house, the blind men approached him and Jesus said to them, "Do you believe that I can do this?"

MEDITATIONS & LESSONS

✦ Christ could question most of our prayers in this fashion.
✦ Truly great things can be accomplished through faith. It is not that faith accomplishes great things, but that God responds to acts of faith.
✦ People with great faith are impelled to spread the word to others.

MATTHEW 10:29

"Are not two sparrows sold for a small coin? Yet not one of them falls to the ground without your Father's knowledge."

MEDITATIONS & LESSONS

✦ Sparrows have little monetary value and yet not one of them falls to the ground without Our Heavenly Father knowing it. If he has concern for sparrows, how much more does he care for us?

MATTHEW 11:7-9

As they were going off, Jesus began to speak to the crowds about John, "What did you go out to the desert to see? A reed swayed by the wind? Then what did you go out to see? Someone dressed in fine clothing? Those who wear fine clothing are in royal palaces. Then why did you go out? To see a prophet?"

Meditations & Lessons

✦   One who can tell us the truth with the authority of a witness and who can, perhaps, even tell us something about the future, will always attract a crowd. Those who come to satisfy their curiosity, yet are unable to accept the truth, may leave, but they are attracted none the less.

✦   A prophet is greater than any natural phenomenon or any rich person because of the truths that he speaks.

✦   We are also drawn to a selfless person, one who lives for others and not for worldly pleasures and possessions.

✦   Poverty, too, will always attract people's interest. We may not understand why someone adopts a life of poverty, but we sense that there is goodness and deep spirituality in such a life and that fascinates us.

Matthew 11:16

"To what shall I compare this generation?"

Meditations & Lessons

✦   This generation can be compared to an adolescent world because it lacks maturity.

✦   People are insecure, unstable, constantly searching, and changing.

✦   This generation is self-centered, selfish, concerned with its rights and with "doing its own thing". It lacks concern for duty and responsibility.

✦   We live in a materialistic age where might makes right, and pleasure, comfort, money, and possessions are the chief concerns.

✦   Rebelliousness is a hallmark of our times. Authority, even that of God, is rejected. There is no sense of history—a rejection of the authority of forebears. There is unrestricted freedom—a rejection of the authority of peers. And there is no concern or responsibility for the future—a rejection of the authority of posterity.

✦ The fruits of such a society are violence, crime, immorality, and ultimately self-destruction. Self-destruction can be manifested through the physical harm of oneself and the loss of one's mental well-being.

MATTHEW 12:3-5

"Have you not read what David did when he and his companions were hungry?...Or have you not read in the law that on the sabbath the priests serving in the temple violate the sabbath and are innocent?"

MEDITATIONS & LESSONS

✦ Sabbath was made for man, and not man for sabbath.

✦ It is not activity or inactivity that counts on the sabbath, but whether our actions are for the honor and the glory of God. Corporal or spiritual works of mercy performed on the sabbath are praiseworthy. Indeed, some priests work harder on Sundays than on other days.

✦ The Lord wants us to observe his law, not man's law. If we are faced with a choice, we should choose that which is moral over that which is legal.

MATTHEW 12:11

"Which one of you who has a sheep that falls into a pit on the sabbath will not take hold of it and lift it out?"

Meditations & Lessons

+ Compare to Matthew 12:3-5.
+ Apparently the laws of the sabbath were such that they would never require a person to take a loss in material possessions.

Matthew 12:26-27

"And if Satan drives out Satan, he is divided against himself; how, then, will his kingdom stand? And if I drive out demons by Beelzebul, by whom do your own people drive them out?"

Meditations & Lessons

+ God does indeed have power over evil.
+ We need help to overcome evil—help from God—and with his help, we, too, can overcome evil.
+ We are to be as innocent as children.

Matthew 12:29

"How can anyone enter a strong man's house and steal his property, unless he first ties up the strong man?"

Meditations & Lessons

+ The power of evil is strong. But the power of Jesus is stronger. He has the power to overcome Satan, and his power is a sign that he is the Messiah.
+ The kingdom of darkness is no match for the Kingdom of God.

MATTHEW 12:34

"You brood of vipers, how can you say good things when you are evil?"

MEDITATIONS & LESSONS

✦   The mouth speaks from the heart. If what we say is good, it comes from our inner goodness, and if what we say is evil, it comes from our inner evil.

✦   Even when a person is successful at disguising his wickedness, over the course of time, his wickedness will still be revealed.

MATTHEW 12:48

"Who is my mother? Who are my brothers?"

MEDITATIONS & LESSONS

✦   It is more important to do God's will and to be holy rather than to be closely related to him by some other bond, for example, as a priest or as a member of a religious order.

✦   The closest bonds of all are Baptism, Confirmation and Eucharist.

✦   We are truly children of God by adoption, brothers and sisters of Christ, heirs to heaven.

MATTHEW 14:31

"O you of little faith, why did you doubt?"

Meditations & Lessons

✦   Jesus' question to Peter after he faltered while walking on the water illustrates that we do not appreciate sufficiently who Jesus is and the power he can exercise in our lives.

✦   We accept human authority more readily than divine authority and yet divine authority is greater than human authority (1 John 5,9). Jesus was exercising divine authority, but Peter's inner weakness made him doubt.

✦   Once we get a little help from God, we think that we can take care of the rest ourselves. Jesus called Peter to get out of the boat and to walk towards him on the water, and Peter obeyed. But after a few steps, Peter forgot that the power to walk on water came from Jesus. He stopped relying on Jesus and began relying on himself, and so he began to sink.

Matthew 15:3

"And why do you break the commandment of God for the sake of your tradition?"

Meditations & Lessons

✦   Often we seem more inclined to obey human laws and customs than we are to observe God's revelation. Indeed, we can favor human laws in order to avoid observing God's laws.

✦   Human laws are always imperfect, and they leave loopholes. Divine laws can be skirted, too, but not for the person of good will. For him, divine laws are a call to perfection.

✦   As we clear away human traditions from our religious practice, we must be certain not to abandon God's law in the process.

Matthew 15:33-34

The disciples said to him, "Where could we ever get enough bread in this deserted place to satisfy such a crowd?" Jesus said to them, "How many loaves do you have?"

Meditations & Lessons

✦   God is willing to accept whatever we have to offer. No matter how small an offering, he will make it adequate. In fact, in multiplying the loaves and fishes, he could have been illustrating the relative value and importance of man's contribution to that of God's in every good work.

✦   God does demand that we offer something, however, and that we be willing to cooperate in good works. He is not going to do it all. And unless we cooperate by an act of our free will, the good work will not be done at all.

✦   The reward for giving is overwhelming—seven heaping baskets of leftovers (verse 37).

Matthew 16:8-9

"You of little faith, why do you conclude among yourselves that it is because you have no bread? Do you not yet understand, and do you not remember the five loaves for the five thousand, and how many wicker baskets you took up?"

Meditations & Lessons

✦   We do not live by bread alone. We live much more by the Word of God, because only God can give life. But we must ponder God's word, or we may misunderstand its significance as the Apostles did in this instance.

✦   The things of this world always seem to us to be of greater importance to us. They come to our minds first, before any thought of God.

✦   Today, we should be able to see the Hand of God at work—through the words and works of the Holy Father and the Church—just as the Apostles should have been able to see it in Christ.

MATTHEW 16:13

"Who do people say that the Son of Man is?"

MEDITATIONS & LESSONS

✦   People are always looking for a "prophet," one who will relieve them of the responsibility for their own lives; one whom they can follow blindly with an assurance that they are right. Those are not the kind of prophets that God gives us. He has given us free will, and he wants us to use it. Amazing how men follow earthly prophets, who tyrannically deprive them of free will!

✦   "The grass always looks greener..." The past always looks better, easier, more secure—and well it should—because we have the benefit of knowing how things have turned out.

✦   Recognition of God in the world, recognition of his will is possible only by virtue of his grace and an act of faith. If we accept these verses of Sacred Scripture (and others that confirm them), we can only know God and his will for us by making an act of faith in his Vicar and in his Church.

✦   Faith is easier when we are young because we need to put our faith in so many people. It is also more fragile in our early years because so many people prove unworthy of our faith. What we need to do is avoid cynicism and not lose faith in everyone and everything simply because a few have not proven worthy. As we grow older, we recognize more readily the human side of the Church. Maybe some Church leaders have betrayed us or led us astray. If we are led by panic rather than faith, we run in different directions seeking to find help which is not there. But if we are patient and do not panic, we recognize in the Church a constant, never failing, divine element, especially in the person of the Vicar of Christ on earth.

MATTHEW 16:15

"But who do you say that I am?"

MEDITATIONS & LESSONS

✦ This is the question for all ages to answer. How each of us responds should set the context for our lives.

✦ If we answer with Peter, "You are the Messiah, the Son of the Living God," we should recognize that Jesus must be central in our lives.

MATTHEW 16:26

"What profit would there be for one to gain the whole world and forfeit his life? Or what can one give in exchange for his life?"

MEDITATIONS & LESSONS

✦ There is nothing—success, money, power, fame—more precious to a person than life because it is a gift of God, a creation in God's own image and likeness, an opportunity to obtain eternal life, perfect happiness.

+   The things of this world are passing. The adage, "You can't take it with you" is true. And indeed, experience shows that material possessions are by no means a guarantee of happiness even in this world. We have only to look at the unhappiness of the rich and famous.

+   The paradox of the Christian life is that "in giving we receive". Life in this world is made happy by giving, and eternal life is made possible only by giving.

MATTHEW 17:17

"O faithless and perverse generation, how long will I be with you? How long will I endure you?"

MEDITATIONS & LESSONS

+   Lack of faithfulness in those who have every reason to believe is a heavy burden for a leader to bear.

+   Faith is a gift from God. We see that, even in the case of Christ, the most beautiful rhetoric (words) and miracles (deeds) were still not sufficiently convincing for the Apostles, not to mention the people.

+   Our choice is between God and man, heaven and earth, spiritual and material. It is a wrenching experience for man to turn away from the "certainties" of the world for the hope and expectation of heaven.

MATTHEW 18:12

"What is your opinion? If a man has a hundred sheep and one of them goes astray, will he not leave the ninety-nine in the hills and go in search of the stray?"

MEDITATIONS & LESSONS

✦ Human beings are often more concerned about their losses, past sins, and missed opportunities rather than their present and future possibilities.

✦ Human beings have a great sympathy for the underdog, the unfortunate. God's sympathy and care extends to those who go astray.

✦ What a blessing it is for any shepherd of souls to have faithful priests and people who do not stray! It takes much more effort to retrieve a soul who has strayed than it takes to retrieve a lost sheep. The brambles of error and unruly emotions have a much stronger hold than the brambles of a bush.

✦ When a person is returning to the fold, we may be forced to "carry" him for a time, be kind, patient, tolerant, and keep an eye on him for a while to see that he stays with the flock and does not wander off again.

MATTHEW 19:16-17

Now someone approached him and said, "Teacher, what good must I do to gain eternal life?" He answered him, "Why do you ask me about the good? There is only One who is good."

MEDITATIONS & LESSONS

✦ God alone is completely good. Goodness is an attribute of his, a sign of divinity. One who keeps the Commandments—which are the guidelines for goodness—is not only following God's will, but also perfecting himself in the image and likeness of God. If we would be perfect, we need to go far beyond mere observance of the Commandments and practice the greatest charity we can.

✦ Regardless of what title a person may have (priest, bishop, etc.), the real leader of a spiritual community will always be the holiest person and will appeal to others just as Christ appeals to others in the Gospel. We may not be able to define holiness or goodness any better than Christ does in this passage, but people can instinctively identify it when they encounter it.

✦ We really should not need to ask what constitutes goodness. Our conscience reveals goodness to us. As Christ points out, the Commandments and all of Sacred Scripture make it clear. We also have the lives of the saints as examples of holiness, as well as the guidance of the Holy Spirit which is found in the Church.

MATTHEW 20:22

"Can you drink the cup that I am going to drink?"

MEDITATIONS & LESSONS

✦ Are you able to unite your will perfectly with that of the Father?

✦ Are you able to face death with equanimity, believing that the life to come is far more valuable than this life?

✦ Do you love not only God, but do you also love truth (God's teaching) and love your neighbors strongly enough that you are willing to die for them?

✦ Are you strong enough in character to die in ignominy and shame, with the world opposed to you?

✦ Can you endure physical suffering?

(*Editor's note:* Physical suffering is caused by bodily pain, and it differs from spiritual suffering. Jesus endured spiritual suffering in the

Garden of Gethsemane before he was arrested. He endured physical suffering at the hands of the Roman soldiers who scourged him, crowned him with thorns, forced him to carry a cross, and crucified him. Bishop Marshall, who died of cancer, well understood the difference between the two forms of suffering.)

MATTHEW 20:29-32

Two blind men were sitting by the roadside, and when they heard that Jesus was passing by, they cried out, "[Lord,] Son of David, have pity on us!"...Jesus stopped and called them and said, "What do you want me to do for you?"

MEDITATIONS & LESSONS

✦ This is an open-hearted invitation from Jesus who is always present to us. What we need is the faith to turn to him.

✦ Powerful as Christ is over the physical world, he has even greater power over the spiritual world. As he indicated in performing so many other miracles, what he really wished to do for us was to increase our faith.

MATTHEW 21:16

"And have you never read the text, 'Out of the mouths of infants and nurslings you have brought forth praise?' "

MEDITATIONS & LESSONS

✦ We must have the innocence of children.

+   We must be humble as children, accepting God's direction as docilely as children accept direction from their parents.

+   God does not look to our worldly accomplishments, how we have come to dominate persons or things in the world. He is more interested in whether or not we have mastered ourselves to become, as he says, like little children.

+   People have a sixth sense for spotting holiness. There is a moral imperative to do so. All through the Gospel, we are told explicitly that ordinary people recognized Christ's holiness. And we sense that the scribes and Pharisees did also, but they were so blinded by a desire for power and by their envy that they could not admit it.

MATTHEW 21:25

"Where was John's baptism from? Was it of heavenly or of human origin?"

MEDITATIONS & LESSONS

+   Jesus asks this question of the chief priests and elders of the people. They wanted to know where Jesus got the authority to perform miracles. And he promised to answer their question if they answered his. When they would not answer his question, it was obvious that they were not ready to hear and accept the truth. Christ supported strongly the example and the teaching of John the Baptist and in Matthew 21:32, he points out that although John came in the way of righteousness, the chief priests and elders refused to believe him. Thus it is possible to be blind to the truth even when the truth is obvious.

+   Human beings are prone to believe only what they want to hear. This confrontation shows that even when they see the truth, human beings can deny it or turn from it because they do not want to act in accordance with it.

♦ God's ways and thoughts are not those of men. So when men agree on a course of action, it is no guarantee that it is God's way. Today, we are seeing a great deal of "follow the leader" theology, in which the leader is not basing his teaching on Sacred Scripture and on the Church, but he is telling us something that sounds good, something we want to hear.

MATTHEW 21:42

"Did you never read in the scriptures:
  'The stone that the builders rejected
  has become the cornerstone;
  by the Lord has this been done,
  and it is wonderful in our eyes'?"

MEDITATIONS & LESSONS

♦ The last shall be first, and the first last.

♦ Success and usefulness in God's Kingdom are not based on worldly criteria.

♦ This is the story of most of the saints and all of the martyrs. They are rejected by this world. But with their death, the Church flourishes.

♦ The truth does strike home. Even though certain people may not wish to accept it, they cannot fail to recognize it.

MATTHEW 22:18

"Why are you testing me, you hypocrites?"

MEDITATIONS & LESSONS

✦   The Pharisees were hypocrites because they pretended to seek God. If they were truly seeking God instead of their own glory, they would have recognized the truth in Christ and realized how fruitless it was to try to trip him.

✦   A person who sins often rationalizes his behavior before he acts. In this way, he is like the Pharisees who pretended to be confused and who asked a fallacious question—"How can we do otherwise?" We cannot obey God and mammon, but both oblige us to do so.

✦   There should never be any real conflicts between Church and state, if both are faithful to their task. When conflicts arise, we should choose the moral course of action, of course, rather than that which is legal.

✦   Just as Christ appeared to be only a human being in the eyes of the Pharisees, so many today see the Church as only a human institution. They do not look beyond the human persons who govern it to the Divine Power that guides it. And so, they ask questions that put the Church very much on the defensive. The questioners are looking for proof that their psychology, sociology, etc. are correct when the only answer is one that depends on faith.

MATTHEW 22:42

"What is your opinion about the Messiah? Whose son is he?"

MEDITATIONS & LESSONS

✦   This is the basic question that every person must confront. It takes an act of faith to say, "He is the son of God" rather than to simply say that he is a human being.

✦ If we truly believe that Christ is God, that makes a world of difference in the way we live. If we reject this idea, that makes a big difference, too. Many accept the fact that Jesus is the son of God, but they accept it with reservations. In a way, this is worse than rejecting Christ because it is acknowledging that he is God, but refusing to act on that knowledge and follow him. These are the lukewarm, whom God will vomit out of his mouth.

MATTHEW 23:17-19

"Blind fools, which is greater, the gold, or the temple that made the gold sacred?...You blind ones, which is greater, the gift, or the altar that makes the gift sacred?"

MEDITATIONS & LESSONS

✦ That which is completely consecrated to the service of God is sacred. If it is not consecrated to him or can be removed (taken back) from him, it is not sacred or completely so (for example, priestly commitment must be absolute).

✦ Spiritual realities are greater than material, unless or until the material has been made sacred.

✦ The altar and the temple represent Jesus and the Father. The adornment represents the gift the worshiper brings to the altar. The worshiper gains his sanctity from the one worshiped, not vice versa. Yet so many think that they are doing God a favor by worshipping him and that this makes them holy. Many believe they know better than the Church what will please God in worship. When Jesus says, "Woe to you, scribes and Pharisees;" he is talking about this kind of behavior.

Matthew 24:45

"Who, then, is the faithful and prudent servant, whom the master has put in charge of his household to distribute to them their food at the proper time?"

Meditations & Lessons

✦   God has placed us on earth in a position of trust. He gives us all the rules for our conduct; in our hearts, in the Commandments, in Christ, and in the Church. And he expects us to fulfill that trust. It is like parents leaving their children at home alone.

✦   Although God knows all things, he is not going to return to this world suddenly and deliberately at the worst possible time for us. Since we believe in his justice and mercy, in fact, we believe that he comes at the best possible time (mercy) or when we have shown our true colors (justice).

✦   The question implies that the good servant is one who is faithful to God, faithful to his fellow human beings, and has a sufficient degree of wisdom. One does not have to be brilliant to understand that God is the Creator, and we are his creatures. We know these things through direct experience and divine revelation, and yet we do not always accept them. Somehow, when it suits our purposes, we are able to find exceptions to what we know to be true and faithful conduct.

Matthew 26:10

"Why do you make trouble for the woman?"

Meditations & Lessons

✦ The context for this question is the beginning of the Passion. A woman anointed Jesus with costly oil and the Disciples were indignant at her extravagance. The question infers that we should not measure spirituality by material standards.

✦ Better to judge a person by his intentions than by the practicality of his words and deeds.

✦ Better not to upset a person who does something in good conscience.

✦ Rather than standing in negative judgment of others, it would be better to concentrate upon ourselves and what we can do for the Lord and our neighbor.

✦ The Disciples claimed it would be better to sell the perfume and give the money to the poor rather than to anoint Christ. Are the Disciples (ourselves) really that interested in giving to the poor, or would we use the money for our own purposes?

Matthew 26:40

"So you could not keep watch with me for one hour?"

Meditations & Lessons

✦ We have all kinds of time for other pursuits, but very little time for prayer.

✦ Prerequisites for prayer are time and attention to God. If we are not willing to give even these, we cannot even begin to develop a spiritual life.

✦　Without prayer we cannot very well lead a virtuous life. The Apostles are told to pray lest they enter into temptation (verse 41—Our Father). They fail to pray; they abandon Christ to his enemies; they even deny that they know him.

✦　Without prayer our devotion is only wishful thinking, "the spirit is willing, but the flesh is weak."

MATTHEW 26:53

"Do you think that I cannot call upon my Father and he will not provide me at this moment with more than twelve legions of angels?"

MEDITATIONS & LESSONS

✦　Victory over the world, on its terms, is no great feat. It is pretty much a matter of mathematics. The larger, more powerful army wins. But victory over the world by means of mind and heart and will has always been acclaimed, even by the world itself.

✦　Frequently, the world seems to overcome God. But it is always a hollow victory because the victory is achieved by a measure of strength, which in turn can be overcome by a greater measure. However, even the greatest measure can never overcome the strength of the Spirit. What does worldly victory prove? Only that the victor is the more powerful one, not that he is just, true, and good. Even in defeat, truth, justice, and goodness, are often, paradoxically, recognized as the victor—even by worldly forces, though grudgingly. This was the case all through the life of Christ.

Matthew 26:55

"Have you come out as against a robber, with swords and clubs to seize me?"

Meditations & Lessons

+ Christ preached nothing but a message of peace. He never gave anyone a reason for thinking that he was given to violence. He never did anything unjust to anyone, and he never bothered the Roman authorities.

+ "Those who live by the sword will perish by the sword." If we place our trust in force, we can be absolutely certain of our downfall because there will always be someone stronger or someone who, by calculation, will deprive us of our strength.

+ Christ had taken nothing from anyone (robber); he had constantly given the wisdom of God, the healing power of God, and his own total being. There was no reason to capture him. He had already freely given himself, "surrendering" from the day He came into the world.

Matthew 27:46

"My God, my God, why have you forsaken me?"

Meditations & Lessons

+ The Father would (could) never forsake the Son. The cry is an expression of a great mystery—how can God be so merciful to men? It is unlikely enough that someone should die for a good man; so how do we explain Christ giving his life for sinners?

✦   The Father had forsaken the Son in that he did not strengthen Christ's followers so that they would have the courage to stand by him. Only Mary, John, and a few women supported Jesus. The Apostles, those whom he had cured, and those who hailed him on Palm Sunday had all deserted him. How easy we find it to rationalize the same kind of conduct.

✦   Christ was innocent of any wrongdoing. Pilate, his wife, and the centurion attest to his innocence, and all three were pagans. It was incredible that so many people who had seen his works and heard his words should turn their backs on Goodness. And yet, we often turn our backs on others on the pretext that the person does not mind, or does not really care or, at least, will not say anything. That is not justification for turning our backs.

Chapter Two

Questions Jesus Asked in the Gospel of Mark

In meditating, it is sometimes helpful to visualize the scene and to place ourselves in it. In Mark's gospel, there is a very compelling incident (10:46-52) in which a blind man named Bartimaeus sat by a roadside begging. When he heard that Jesus was near, he called out to him. Immediately, people in the crowd rebuked Bartimaeus and told him to be quiet. But Bartimaeus called even more loudly, and Jesus heard Bartimaeus and instructed his disciples to bring Bartimaeus to him. Perhaps, the blind man had second thoughts and hesitated, but now the mood of the crowd changed, and he was urged to have courage and approach Jesus. When he did so, Jesus asked, "What do you want me to do for you?

Bishop Marshall points out that Jesus asks the same question of us.

So in our meditation, we can put ourselves in place of Bartimaeus. We are on the road of life, and there is something we lack, an obstacle that interferes with our desire to be a disciple or something we need to successfully complete our journey. Suddenly, we are in the presence of One who has all power, one who can change our lives, cast out our darkness and replace it with his light. We want to call out to him, but there are inner voices which tell us to be silent. They are voices which fear change, voices of pride which say we do not need help, voices of despair that say we are not worthy to be helped.

Yet, we know we are in the presence of the Master who loves us, and so we summon the courage to approach Jesus and hear his question, "What do you want me to do for you?"

It is a question filled with love, a question which reveals how much Jesus wants to reach out to us and help us. And it is asked by one who really has the power to act in our lives.

Like the blind Bartimaeus, we can respond, "Master, I want to see." We can tell the Lord that we want to be healed of spiritual blindness or healed of some problem that comes from spiritual blindness, such as a lack of forgiveness or a resentment or an inability to love another. Or we might ask Jesus for some other important spiritual good that is lacking in our lives.

In any case, in our meditation, we should realize that Jesus did not come just to heal Bartimaeus. He also came to change our lives by calling us into a closer relationship with him so that we can recognize that he is indeed the way and the truth and the life.

Mark 2:5-9

When Jesus saw their faith, he said to the paralytic, "Child, your sins are forgiven." Now some of the scribes were sitting there asking themselves, "Why does this man speak that way? He is blaspheming. Who but God alone can forgive sins?" Jesus immediately knew in his mind what they were thinking to themselves, so he said, "Why are you thinking such things in your hearts? Which is easier, to say to the paralytic, 'Your sins are forgiven,' or to say, 'Rise pick up your bed and walk?'"

Meditations & Lessons:

♦ When a person does not voice his questions or opinions, he must have some degree of guilt or at least some fear or some uncertainty. He may not want to even have his questions answered.

♦ The doubters were unable to see Jesus for what he was and for what he was doing. They had some kind of an emotional block. Jesus could not really respond to their doubts with a rational argument, so he used miracles in hopes of stirring them. When miracles produced little effect over the course of time, it became evident that the emotional block was a deep prejudice, where they did not recognize Jesus as Messiah.

♦ Unless we ask the right questions, we will never receive the right answers. If we make up our mind before we know the facts, we will be unable to learn and to discover the truth. The Pharisees had already decided that Jesus was not God and could not forgive sins, so it was impossible for them to ask the right questions in order to discover the truth.

♦ By his own question and miracle, Christ brought the Pharisees to the heart of the matter. They did not want to recognize him as

Messiah, even though he demonstrated his power. Indeed, Jesus' question, "Which is easier..." demonstrates the ease with which he exercised miraculous power. The Pharisees were amazed, but because of the depth of their prejudice they could not be opened to the possibility that he might be God.

MARK 2:19

"Can the wedding guests fast while the bridegroom is with them?"

MEDITATIONS & LESSONS:

+   The Disciples of Jesus were criticized because they did not fast. But Jesus points out that there is a time to fast and a time not to fast. If one does not feel well, he does not show it at a wedding feast. It is not simply a matter of self-mortification; it is a joyous response to the host who produces such a happy atmosphere. This is especially true of Jesus and those who associate with him. As long as he is with us, we cannot very well be negative about anything.

+   The wedding party is not going to continue endlessly. Neither will we always feel Christ's presence. Jesus is always present to us, but the cares of the world frequently push him into the background. At these times, we suffer and we need faith to bring us through the "dark night of the soul". Only a more conscious awareness of Jesus' presence will bring back our peace and joy.

MARK 2:25-26

"Have you never read what David did when he was in need and he and his companions were hungry? How he went into the house

of God when Abiathar was high priest and ate the bread of offer-
ing that only the priests could lawfully eat, and shared it with his
companions?"

MEDITATIONS & LESSONS:

✦   Love of neighbor supercedes all other duties except love of God.
By and large, they are the same. Of course, it is neither love of self nor
love of neighbor that causes one to act contrary to the adoration of God.
We are not loving God when we deny someone's need simply in order to
stand on ceremony.

✦   The Eucharist is not primarily for adoration, but for strengthen-
ing the spiritual life of those who receive it. In the case of the Temple
loaves, the bread did both. The presence of the Eucharist in us allows us
to adore and to be spiritually strengthened.

✦   When we are in need, the best food of all is the Eucharist and the
Word of God.

MARK 3:4

"Is it lawful to do good on the sabbath rather than to do evil, to
save life rather than to destroy it?"

MEDITATIONS & LESSONS:

✦   "If you say that you love God and scorn your neighbor, you are
a liar" (1 John 4:20). "As long as you did it for one of these least brethren,
you did it for me" (Mt: 25,40). There are exceptions to every rule—and
Jesus tells us that the sabbath was made for man and not man for the sabbath. "That is why the Son of Man is Lord even of the sabbath."

✦   We are forbidden to use an evil means to attain a good end, for example, neglecting a neighbor on the sabbath in order to serve God. Obviously, we have an obligation to serve our neighbor and to serve God. Therefore, neither responsibility should be taken lightly or be used as an excuse to avoid fulfilling the other duty.

✦   The claim that we are keeping one Commandment scrupulously can never be used as an excuse for violating another Commandment. We cannot neglect our neighbor on the pretense of obeying our parents.

Mark 3:22-23

The scribes who had come from Jerusalem said, "He is possessed by Beelzebul," and "By the prince of demons he drives out demons." Summoning them, he began to speak to them in parables, "How can Satan drive out Satan?"

Meditations & Lessons:

✦   We cannot gain dominion over evil in the world unless we develop a life of virtue with the help of God's grace. Neither an evil person nor a person of merely human goodness is capable of conquering evil. Only God can accomplish this.

✦   Through the power of God, all things are possible; nothing can overcome us in an absolute sense. Evil cannot contend with goodness. It is our lack of goodness or our desire to overcome evil by our own power without God, that brings about sin in our lives.

Mark 3:33-35

"Who are my mother and [my] brothers?" And looking around at

those seated in the circle he said, "Here are my mother and my brothers. [For] whoever does the will of God is my brother and sister and mother."

MEDITATIONS & LESSONS:

✦ In the mind of Jesus, God is the Father of all. Our claim upon him is equal to his very own mother and relatives. Obviously, there was a very special relationship between son and mother, but, although we are not her equal in holiness, we are equally the concern of Christ. We, too, would have a more special relationship with him, if we were more holy. We are the ones who hold up the development of such a relationship.

✦ As followers of Christ, especially those of us who are his priests, we should be able to ask and answer this question as he did. It should be particularly easy for us, if our parents have passed on. The people entrusted to our pastoral care are, or should be, family to us, just as our natural brothers and sisters. They deserve as much of our time, energy and love as we give to our own families.

MARK 4:21

"Is a lamp brought in to be placed under a bushel basket or under a bed, and not to be placed on a lampstand?"

MEDITATIONS & LESSONS:

✦ Jesus came into the world in order to give light to the world, to reveal the will of the Father, to bring truth and understanding to men.

✦ The calling of every follower of Christ is the same, especially his priest. We are not necessarily capable of making "infallible" statements on every moral issue that comes before us. But at the least, we should have the moral courage to proclaim the Gospel itself and to let others apply it, if we are not capable of the application. It is understandable that we might not have the competence for application, but proclamation only requires closeness to Christ and knowledge of his message, which are gained from prayer and spiritual reading.

✦ As followers of Christ, we are not to be concerned about the powerful brightness of the light or whether or not the light touches everyone. We leave that to God's providence. But God does depend on human instruments to proclaim his message. Our task is to be consistent, courageous, and in contact with people, so that God's message is proclaimed.

Mark 4:30

"To what shall we compare the kingdom of God, or what parable can we use for it?"

Meditations & Lessons:

✦ Christ goes on to use the parable of the mustard seed to explain the Kingdom of God, but even this parable does not explain it adequately. Vatican Council II calls the Church a great mystery and points out many images that can be used to describe it, but admittedly these images are all inadequate.

✦ The Kingdom of God is a spiritual reality, of course, and therein lies the problem. Only faith can bring a degree of understanding, but even faith is inadequate because in trying to understand the Kingdom of God through analogy or comparison, the human mind must use the images and terms of this world—and the Kingdom of God is not of this world.

+ For now we have settled on the People of God as the most appropriate image of the Church. But we should not ignore any of the images or parables that Christ uses. We can learn much about the Kingdom from each one of them.

MARK 4:37-40

A violent squall came up and waves were breaking over the boat, so that it was already filling up. Jesus was in the stern, asleep on a cushion. They woke him and said to him, "Teacher, do you not care that we are perishing?" He woke up, rebuked the wind...Then he asked them, "Why are you terrified? Do you not yet have faith?"

MEDITATIONS & LESSONS:

+ If we have full faith in God and in his teachings (eternal life), there is never any reason to fear the evils of this world.

+ It is not unusual for a person to be afraid in this world. There are many things that can cause fear in us. Jesus recognizes this. The important word in his question is "why." The answer that we all must generally confess is, "I am not prepared for death." The only evil we should really fear is sin. But most of us are on friendly terms with sin, even when we do not actually commit sin. Often we are more comfortable with sin in the world than with virtue. We know that this should not be and that is why we are afraid of death.

+ The Apostles had faith in Christ, but their hope was for some sort of success in this world. They saw that hope being dashed by the storm. They looked to God for help in this world. They did not as yet aspire for union with God in the world to come.

MARK 5:30

"Who has touched my clothes?"

MEDITATIONS & LESSONS:

✦ It was not that someone had touched his garments, but the reason why they were touched and the result of the action. A woman who had hemorrhaged for twelve years believed that if she touched his garments, she would be healed. She did touch his garments, and she was healed. The woman's spirit of faith and supplication were somehow evident in her touch. So our faith, hope, and love must be genuine if we are to touch the heart of Christ in our prayer.

✦ Perhaps the Apostles did not need miracles for themselves, but often in the Gospel, the faith of the people outshines the faith of the Apostles. The same can be the case in our own day.

MARK 5:38-39

When they arrived at the house of the synagogue official, he caught sight of a commotion, people weeping and wailing loudly. So he went in and said to them, "Why this commotion and weeping? The child is not dead but asleep."

MEDITATIONS & LESSONS:

✦ At the time of a person's death, there is no need for uncontrolled grief unless we have been responsible in some way—by our action or lack of action—to help the person save his soul. In this event, we should truly lament what has happened. In any case, the person is "in the hands of God".

✦ Most often our mourning is for ourselves, for our loss rather than for any loss the dead person has incurred. In fact, the dead person has great gain. Our mourning would not be nearly so great, if we had done everything within our power to help that person to holiness of life. In that event, we would be calm, possessed even by a subdued joy.

✦ Often it can happen that a display of emotion at the time of death is for the benefit of others. We do what we are expected to do. We are playing to the world instead of being ourselves. Those who are truly and deeply grieved usually seek solitude.

MARK 7:18-19

"Are even you likewise without understanding? Do you not realize that everything that goes into a person from outside cannot defile, since it enters not the heart but the stomach and passes out into the latrine?" (Thus he declared all foods clean.)

MEDITATIONS & LESSONS:

✦ Eating something may make one physically sick, but it can have no moral or spiritual effect of itself. Moral and spiritual virtue or fault come from within one's being. "What comes out of a person, that is what defiles. From within people, from their hearts, come evil thoughts, unchastity, theft, murder, adultery, greed, malice, deceit, licentiousness, envy, blasphemy, arrogance, folly. All these evils come from within and they defile."

MARK 8:12

"Why does this generation seek a sign? Amen, I say to you, no sign will be given to this generation."

Meditations & Lessons:

✦   We have enough signs already. The Jews had all the signs of the Old Testament. We have many more still.

✦   Why does this generation ask for a sign? It is clear in the Gospel that the people of Christ's time did not easily accept signs. They wanted concrete, tangible action and results. They could not see beyond the physical, due to the hardness of their hearts. They could not understand the parables. They could not even see that the power of God is present in a miracle (Mark 8:17-18).

Mark 8:17-19

"Why do you conclude that it is because you have no bread? Do you not yet understand or comprehend? Are your hearts hardened? Do you have eyes and not see, ears and not hear? And do you not remember, when I broke the five loaves for the five thousand, how many wicker baskets full of fragments you picked up?"

Meditations & Lessons:

✦   God will provide! Christ had just fed five thousand people with a few loaves and fishes! God takes care of the birds of the air and the flowers of the field, and he will take care of us. What we need to do is to "take care of him", by carrying out his will in the world. Then, whether we live or die—that is up to him—all will be well. Seek first the Kingdom of God and his justice!

✦   If our hearts are hardened, we are unable to see the truth even when it is right in front of us. The Disciples apparently did not comprehend Christ's power even though they witnessed it.

MARK 8:22-23

When they arrived at Bethsaida, they brought to him a blind man and begged him to touch him...Putting spittle on his eyes he laid his hands on him and asked, "Do you see anything?"

MEDITATIONS & LESSONS:

✦ Only through the grace and power of Christ will we ever be able to see anything with a spiritual, eternal perspective. Archbishop Jadot makes a great distinction between knowing (faith) and understanding (mentalities). The same distinction can be made with regard to our knowing and understanding God, to our knowing and understanding his teaching.

✦ Spiritual insight is refined as Jesus' works in our life. In this incident, Jesus restored sight to a blind man. When he asked this question, the blind man revealed that he could see but that his sight was distorted. Jesus continued to work with him until he could see clearly.

MARK 8:27

"Who do people say that I am?"

MEDITATIONS & LESSONS:

✦ It really does not matter what men say about God, even the wisest of men. We should give credence to what God says about himself—as long as we are assured that it is God who speaks.

✦ It is not important what others think, it is important what God thinks. Certitude does not come from people, it comes from God. But it is important what we think. Who do we think Jesus is? And who do we say he is?

◆   It is necessary to listen to people, if we are to know how to deal with them. It is important to know what they think and to understand their mind-set, if we are to approach them properly.

◆   Human beings are always going to be limited in their imagination and ideals, even though it is theoretically possible for the soul to know the infinite. Man's knowledge depends upon the senses, and therefore, it is difficult to go beyond material explanations, even when one witnesses miracles. Instead of being convinced of a supernatural intervention, we are merely left wondering about the strange occurrence.

MARK 8:29

"But who do you say that I am?"

◆   People who are close to Jesus have a clearer and deeper understanding of him. Thus, while some people thought Jesus was Elijah or John the Baptist or one of the other prophets, Jesus expected his disciples to have a better understanding. Indeed, Peter understood and answered, "You are the Messiah."

◆   The closer we get to Jesus, the better we get to know him. And as we get to know him, we gain a greater understanding of what it means that he is Messiah and Lord.

MARK 8:34-37

"Whoever wishes to come after me must deny himself, take up his cross, and follow me. For whoever wishes to save his life will lose it, but whoever loses his life for my sake and that of the

gospel will save it. What profit is there for one to gain the whole world and forfeit his life? What could one give in exchange for his life?"

MEDITATIONS & LESSONS:

✦ When all is said and done, the only thing that is essential to us is life itself. We do need things that sustain life, and there are other things that we find very helpful. But even these things are of no value compared to life itself, because we can be deprived of them (die) and life still goes on. What is important is that we keep life for all eternity rather than have eternal death.

✦ Nothing in this world can compare either to the natural life that God has given to us or the supernatural life that we receive in baptism. Everything else is temporary, passing and may give pleasure to the body, but not necessarily happiness to the soul. There is nothing in this world, no matter how marvelous, that can compare to life.

✦ Man cannot give anything in return for his life. In a sense, life is all he has; and even life belongs to God, not to man. Life is priceless; no money can buy it or replace it. We have only one life. It is imperative that we use it well.

✦ The only way to use one's life and to save it, is the same process. "Take up your cross and follow me." Follow in the way and the truth and the life of Christ. This way quite often brings pain, suffering, and dying to self, but it also brings peace, joy, and satisfaction of doing God's will.

MARK 9:19

"O faithless generation, how long will I be with you? How long will I endure you?"

MEDITATIONS & LESSONS:

♦ If a school teacher often asks the same question, how painful it must have been for Jesus to work so hard to explain God's word to human beings and have so little understanding on their part? They were good people, but either they were listening only for what they wanted to hear, or they lacked understanding because they accepted Christ's words only in terms of their own limited background, unable to accept any truly new emphasis.

♦ Time is always short. There is no time to be wasted—not in the sense that we must be engaged in a rush of activity, but in the sense that God wills all men to be saved. The slower we are to learn about Christ and to act on his word, the longer it takes to reach others and we may never reach those whom we should. And in so many instances, we never do appreciate Christ's word sufficiently well that we act upon it with vigor.

MARK 9:33

"What were you arguing about on the way?"

MEDITATIONS & LESSONS:

♦ We should discuss nothing without bringing God into the conversation—at least by invoking his presence and by using his words.

♦ Jesus asked this question shortly after Peter, James and John had witnessed his transfiguration and just after Jesus had told them that he would be put to death and rise three days later. But instead of discussing these momentous things, the Disciples were arguing about who was the greatest among themselves. This may be the best example of leaving God out of the conversation.

✦ The conversations of human beings are so often non-productive or counterproductive as in this case. Conversations are a benefit to sociability, but they are also "time-killers;" they are used for talking uncharitably about other people; they are of worldly matters that might be sinful and at best do not advance the cause of Christ.

MARK 9:50

"Salt is good, but if salt becomes insipid, with what will you restore its flavor? Keep salt in yourselves and you will have peace with one another."

MEDITATIONS & LESSONS:

✦ Human beings are good, but if we lose our humility, which gives us a true understanding of our relationship to God, how can we be the persons we ought to be?

✦ If we fail to accept and use God's grace, we know that our good human nature has been so weakened that we cannot for long avoid a sinful life.

✦ A true understanding of our relation to God and God's grace within us will enable us to understand our relationship to those around us and give us the power to act accordingly, in love and charity, so that we may live in peace.

MARK 10:3

"What did Moses command you?"

MEDITATIONS & LESSONS:

✦   Christ stands by the prophets, as in the story of Lazarus—if they will not listen to Moses and the prophets, neither will they listen if a man should rise from the dead.

✦   Although some instructions of the prophets may have been superceded by the New Testament (as in this case, where Jesus discusses the Jewish law concerning divorce), it is clear that the Old Testament is recognized by Christ as the Word of God and a Word that is to be obeyed.

✦   There is no question that Christ sets himself above Moses, and therefore, above all the other prophets as well. Christ did not come to destroy the law, but he did come to fulfill it, to have the final word.

MARK 10:17-18

As he was setting out on a journey, a man ran up, knelt down before him, and asked him, "Good teacher, what must I do to inherit eternal life?" Jesus answered him, "Why do you call me good? No one is good but God alone."

MEDITATIONS & LESSONS:

✦   Goodness is a sign of godliness. It begins with the keeping of the Commandments (as Jesus tells the rich young man in this instance), but goes far beyond that. Goodness begins with love and adoration for God and extends to charity toward men. Goodness includes all of the kindness and consideration that Jesus had for the Father and those with whom he came in contact.

✦   Cardinal Cushing used to speak of "Good Pope John." Many could speak of Cardinal Cushing in the same way. It would seem that their primary characteristic is understanding, compassion, resulting in kindness.

MARK 10:38

"Can you drink the cup that I drink or be baptized with the baptism with which I am baptized?"

MEDITATIONS & LESSONS

+ No one is able to drink the cup of suffering that Christ drinks unless he is strengthened by God's grace, but that strength will be given to chosen witnesses.

+ If we wish the focus of our lives to be serving Jesus, we must be willing to suffer with him.

+ This could be used as a citation to prove the validity of baptism of blood.

MARK 10:51

"What do you want me to do for you?"

MEDITATIONS & LESSONS:

+ The blind man had called out, "Jesus, son of David, have pity on me." Jesus recognizes the man's great faith and rewards it. He does not perform the miracles so much to demonstrate his power as to demonstrate the power and the need for faith.

+ Although there are few verses in the Gospel that explicitly refer to Christ's divinity, this question and the context in which it was placed, surely indicate a strong conviction of divinity in the mind of Christ. It was obvious that the blind man was seeking more than money.

✦   The question is surely a memorable one, and one that we should keep constantly in mind. It is an offer of service and possibly more—not from us to God, but from God to us—if our faith is sufficiently strong.

MARK 11:17

"Is it not written:
*   'My house shall be called a house of prayer for all*
peoples?' "

MEDITATIONS & LESSONS:

✦   There should be something prayerful about everything that takes place in Church. It is God's "house."

✦   Prayer is our first obligation to God. The fact that he is infinite and we are creatures must always be in the forefront of our minds.

✦   "All the nations"—anyone who wishes to pray to God is welcome in the Church to do so, if they find it an atmosphere conducive to prayer. This is a basic "right" that goes beyond one's particular religious beliefs.

MARK 11:30

"Was John's baptism of heavenly or of human origin?"

MEDITATIONS & LESSONS:

✦   We are fortunate that, in responding to similar questions today (for example, Charismatics, miracles), we have the divinely-founded

Church to ultimately give us guidance. The Pharisees had God's guidance, but it does not compare to the special guidance which he gives the Church.

   ✦   Even if the Pharisees were aided by the Holy Spirit, it would not have helped them because they were more political than spiritual in their judgments. Their decision not to answer was based on their personal prejudice and on the temper of the crowd. We still are faced with this temptation in our own time.

Mark 12:15-16

"Why are you testing me?...Whose image and inscription is this?"

Meditations & Lessons:

   ✦   This is an instance where the Pharisees and Herodians were trying to trap Jesus in an attempt to gather evidence against him. They asked Jesus whether it was lawful to pay taxes to Caesar. Jesus asked for a coin and showed them Caesar's face. He told them, "Repay to Caesar what is Caesar's and to God what is God's." The answer amazed them because they did not realize that Jesus always had the answer, indeed that Jesus is the answer.

   ✦   We should not test the Lord our God, as we do so often by our presumptuous, sinful conduct. "God saves everyone"—does he? "Love and do what you please" all depends on what one means by "love," for example, "If you love me, keep my commandments...Teach them to observe all things whatsoever I have commanded you."

   ✦   "Repay to Caesar what belongs to Caesar," Jesus says. We have no right or obligation to fail to support the legitimate government by taxes and other means, even though we might not particularly care for the government. Although violent revolution might be technically justified in some conditions, we should be ready for persecution and arrest, even if we are protesting some injustice of the state.

✦   Putting Christ to the test is reversing the roles of God and man. We have a nerve to question him; we are making ourselves to be gods. In addition, it is an insult to God to expect that he is going to offend against public order, undermine legitimate authority, which is presumed to be acting for the common good, unless proven otherwise.

MARK 12:24

"Are you not misled because you do not know the scriptures or the power of God?"

MEDITATIONS & LESSONS:

✦   When making decisions, we are always in danger of being wrong if we do not take into account God's teachings on the matter.

✦   In thinking of God, there is always the danger that we will consider him in human terms. We may grant that he is great and powerful, but still many think of him in terms of being less than divine.

✦   Some ignore Scripture as a source of knowledge. Even many Catholics do so on the grounds that others do not believe in Scripture. What difference does that make? The important thing is to know the truth. We do not necessarily need to use Scripture as a proof to others. But Scripture should be the main source of assurance for a believer.

✦   The only one who can properly understand Scripture and the power of God is God himself. But he has given this power to the Church, to be voiced through Peter, the Apostles, and their successors. It is the height of presumption to think that the individual is superior to the authority established by God to interpret his Word. This would be to claim divine power for the individual.

MARK 12:26

"As for the dead being raised, have you not read in the Book of Moses, in the passage about the bush, how God told him, 'I am the God of Abraham, [the] God of Isaac, and [the] God of Jacob'?"

MEDITATIONS & LESSONS:

✦ After death, true life begins. Awesome as the gift of life on earth may be, we can have no idea what the life of heaven is. But Christ assures us that there is such a thing as everlasting life, living with him and with all those who have ever lived.

✦ Jesus was responding to a question from the Sadducees about a woman who had been widowed seven times and to which of her seven husbands she would be married at the resurrection. The Sadducees did not believe in resurrection, and Jesus tells them and all who do not believe in life after death that they are misled.

MARK 12:35-37

"How do the scribes claim that the Messiah is the son of David? ...David himself calls him 'lord'; so how is he his son?"

MEDITATIONS & LESSONS:

✦ The scribes were the only people who could read and write, the only ones who had gone to school. They knew Scripture backward and forward, but they used it only for their human advantage, taking the word out of context or not considering Scripture as a whole. Surely Scripture says that the Christ is of the line of David, but if David calls the Christ his Lord, there must be some mystery involved. Christ pointed this out to the scribes and the people. The people could see that the scribes were caught short, but they themselves were uneducated and incapable of coming up with an answer. Whereas the scribes were unwilling to examine the question because they were afraid of what the answer might be, and it would destroy every preconceived notion they had.

MARK 13:2

"Do you see these great buildings? There will not be one stone left upon another that will not be thrown down."

MEDITATIONS & LESSONS:

✦   Man-made marvels, as impressive as they may be, are still only man-made marvels. They are subject to destruction just as every material thing is subject to destruction.

✦   Jesus demonstrates his prophetic powers because the Romans did destroy the Temple in 70 A.D. When we put our faith in human things, we are likely to be disappointed.

MARK 14:3-6

When he was in Bethany reclining at table in the house of Simon the leper, a woman came with an alabaster jar of perfumed oil....She broke the alabaster jar and poured it on his head. There were some who were indignant. "Why has there been this waste of perfumed oil? It could have been sold for more than three hundred days' wages and the money given to the poor."...Jesus said, "Let her alone. Why do you make trouble for her?"

MEDITATIONS & LESSONS:

✦   We, too, tend to be critical of those who are doing good for the same reason, that their time, energy and money could be spent on better causes. We are especially critical, when their good intentions lead them to a certain excess and objective waste.

✦   We would be better advised to join the charitable person and correct any imprudence by gently showing the person the error of her ways, rather than to stand on the sidelines withholding our own charity from the poor and uncharitably criticizing those who do help. The very least we can do is to leave the person alone. "Let her alone. Why do you trouble her?"

MARK 14:37

"Simon, are you asleep? Could you not keep watch for one hour?"

MEDITATIONS & LESSONS:

✦   We never know when we are most needed by other people. Possibly they can tell us later, but sometimes there are crises in a person's life that are not always outwardly apparent. Or as in the case of Christ and the Apostles, we think that a person is so strong that he does not need our help.

✦   God never asks us for anything beyond our ability to give. Surely he was not asking very much of the Apostles. Quite often we find ourselves expecting God to place more serious demands upon us, and we neglect to do the easier, day-to-day acts of charity toward our neighbor that are more in keeping with what he ordinarily asks of us.

✦   Prayer is often only "watching with him". Many times there is little or nothing to say, or we are simply too tired. We ought to be listening more often than we do. Silence, absence, thinking of the other person are important elements of any friendship. More than words or actions, it is the spiritual presence, the moral support, and the knowledge that someone else truly understands that is important. If we can help when a friend is experiencing difficulty, our friend will be grateful, but in many instances we cannot change the situation for the other person. What the person needs is our company, our presence, our concern, and our support.

MARK 14:48

"Have you come out as against a robber, with swords and clubs, to seize me?"

MEDITATIONS & LESSONS:

✦   Christ was not trying to take anything away from the Jews, not even from the Pharisees. He was trying to give them a revelation from the Father. True, if they accepted it, they would be forced to change themselves, but that would be for their own good, as well as for the good of others. Vatican Council II is a catalyst in that same way for us.

✦   Christ had voluntarily engaged the Pharisees in debate on several occasions. If they wished to discuss something with him, he would have consented. The capture at Gethsemane is another sign that the Sanhedrin had made up its mind concerning Christ's guilt.

+   No one could convict Christ of sin, and yet they treated him as a criminal. Everything he did, he did publicly and openly. In private, all he did was pray and talk to his apostles. But if there is no sinful or illegal action that one can point to, arrest is completely out of order. This is our objection to repressive regimes in the present day.

MARK 15:34

"My God, my God, why have you forsaken me?"

MEDITATIONS & LESSONS:

+   These words remind us of the words at Gethsemane, "Let this chalice pass from me...Not my will but thine be done." Surely from a human standpoint, the Father could have accomplished his will in a more convenient fashion than to allow Christ to be put to death by crucifixion. And so, the words seem to echo the humanity of Christ more than his divinity. On the other hand, the Gospel and the words of Christ are for us—to help us appreciate how God loves us. If Christ went through his passion and death stoically, we could hardly appreciate how much he loved us.

CHAPTER THREE

Questions Jesus Asked in the Gospel of Luke

I n Luke's Gospel, we get further insights into Jesus' human personality. We see that Jesus expects people to recognize what is obvious to him. For example, as a boy, he leaves the group he had traveled with to Jerusalem. When his parents finally find him preaching in the temple, he is surprised that they did not look in the temple in the first place.

We also see his frustration with his disciples. They argue about who is greatest. They fall asleep while he is experiencing a terrible ordeal in Gethsemane. They do not seem to recognize all the Scripture has said about him. In many ways, they fail to realize just who is in their midst.

Frequently, Jesus asks questions which cause the Disciples to examine themselves—why faith is lacking or why they are troubled or why they have failed to do something he asked. Through these questions we come to understand one of the aspects of our role in our relationship with him. We are called to self-examination because self-examination leads to growth.

We, too, must answer the questions that Jesus asks. We must place ourselves in his presence and listen to his voice. To many of his questions, we can answer that we are sinners, that we need more faith. We need to rely on him rather than on self. Other questions that he asks reveal to us the immensity of God's love and care for us—a reality which we too often fail to recognize. But it is a reality that we grasp more and more as we spend time with him in meditation, listening to his questions and giving our answers.

LUKE 2:48-49

When his parents saw him, they were astonished, and his mother said to him, "Son, why have you done this to us? Your father and I have been looking for you with great anxiety." And he said to them, "Why were you looking for me? Did you not know that I must be in my Father's house?"

MEDITATIONS & LESSONS

✦   It is as natural for Jesus to be in the Temple (his Father's house) as it is for us to be in our homes. The question comes in response to his mother after she and Joseph had been looking for Jesus for three days and finally found him in the Temple. At first, it may seem to be the petulant response of a twelve-year-old, but on second reading, Jesus seems to be saying, 'Why were you looking in other places for me? Surely you should have come directly here. You should have known that this was the place to find me.'

✦ It is true that we must make the rounds of our parish as Christ traveled the length and breadth of Palestine, but we must be in our Father's House often, too, at prayer. Surely we must spend more time there than we spend in places of amusement or recreation. How often do people find their priest in the Church today? Would they really think to look for him there? What is their common picture of the priest? If they were describing what he does, would they at least paint a word-picture of him at prayer?

✦ Christ has a sense of obligation about being in his Father's House. So should we. If we think that there is benefit for the people to be there for Mass and prayer, we must set the example.

✦ Although our emphasis on the corporal and spiritual works of mercy today is appropriate, we must never forget the time that Christ spent in the temple, the synagogue, at prayer (all night, before many miracles, Gethsemane). Surely his day was filled with good works, but there is every evidence that his nights (no electricity, no books, no television or radio) were given to long hours of prayer.

LUKE 5:21-22

Then the scribes and Pharisees began to ask themselves, "Who is this who speaks blasphemies? Who but God alone can forgive sins?" Jesus knew their thoughts and said to them in reply, "What are you thinking in your hearts?"

MEDITATIONS & LESSONS

✦ Ironically, the scribes and Pharisees answered the question of who Jesus was when they said, "Who but God alone can forgive sins?" But they denied the reality of their experience because their minds were closed to the fact that he is the Messiah.

   ✦   The Disciples, too, may have been questioning in their hearts because their faith was not sufficiently great. They were doubters rather than believers. They wanted to believe in the greatness of Jesus, but when he acted with supernatural authority, such as forgiving sin, it was too much for them.

   ✦   If there is something on our mind, we should say it. That allows us to face the issue directly with the other person involved. Permitting the other person to respond, eliminates many misunderstandings and frees both parties from being the potential targets of rumors and nuances.

Luke 5:23

"Which is easier, to say, 'Your sins are forgiven,' or to say, 'Rise and walk'?"

Meditations & Lessons

   ✦   If one has both of these powers—to forgive and to provide favors—by all odds, it is more difficult to exercise forgiveness. It is easy to provide favors because they make us look important in the eyes of others and bring consolation and satisfaction. From a human standpoint, forgiveness does not do much for the forgiver. It may reap resentment instead of gratitude from others unless we are very careful. However, from a spiritual standpoint, it can do wonders.

   ✦   Forgiveness is more important from the standpoint of the recipient. Sin is death; forgiveness brings life. Whereas, being crippled may bring inconvenience—even great inconvenience—but life is still present, and therefore, hope and love are present, too.

Luke 5:34

"Can you make the wedding guests fast while the bridegroom is with them?"

Meditations & Lessons

✦ Religion does not demand that we do what is unnatural. When there is cause for celebration and joy, we should celebrate and be joyful. This should always be true in our worship. Since the Mass is the re-presentation of the death and resurrection of Jesus, it should always be celebrated in the spirit of Easter.

✦ On the other hand, we live in the midst of the world where the Lord is present, but most often goes unrecognized. In these circumstances, surely we are going to suffer (fast) and have many lackluster days. It is union with the Lord in prayer at Mass, doing his work (corporal and spiritual works of mercy) that we come alive. So there need be no day in which we are without the bridegroom, unless we deliberately neglect him. Peace, joy, and celebration are possible to us at all times, if we seek the Lord.

Luke 6:3

"Have you not read what David did when he and those [who were] with him were hungry?"

Meditations & Lessons

✦ Man-made restrictions on human beings, even those made in the name of religion, are not for that reason always good and unchangeable.

Usually the original intention was good; the regulation was meant to be helpful to people for a time in certain circumstances. But only God-made laws are good always and forever.

 ◆ Unfortunately, we can distort this principle of mutability in man-made laws in two directions. Some divinize human laws—they give divine authority to man-made laws. Others humanize divine law. So they take divine law, which is always good and unchangeable, and treat it as if it were man-made law. In our present day, the Church is trying to eliminate human laws that have been "divinized." This is difficult for people to understand, but a good and necessary step. However, the situation becomes highly complicated and dangerous to faith, when some sophisticates go to the other extreme and "throw out the baby with the bath water" by humanizing the divine law until "anything goes". In such a situation, the only safe-guide to follow is the Pope and the Bishops in union with him.

LUKE 6:9

"I ask you, is it lawful to do good on the sabbath rather than to do evil, to save life rather than to destroy it?"

MEDITATIONS & LESSONS

 ◆ Obviously, in our Christian era, it is right every day to do good and to save life. Any other view would be alien to us.

 ◆ Regardless of the circumstances—even to attain a good end—we are never to destroy or harm another. Still, we can see the errors that human beings can make. Prior to Christ, the Pharisees would allow evil, rather than break the sabbath. Today, we commit evil actions in order to obtain "good" ends. For instance, we perform abortions out of concern for the mother's convenience or for preventing an unwanted child.

LUKE 6:32

"For if you love those who love you, what credit is that to you?"

MEDITATIONS & LESSONS

✦ If we return goodness for goodness, it is only justice, not charity, even though justice is a virtue and lack of justice is a vice. Justice is giving to another what is due or owed to him. It is no great credit to us then to be just, but going beyond justice—to love—is what God asks of us.

✦ Credit really belongs to the person who initiates a friendship. As St. John and St. Paul tell us, God loved us first, and Christ died for us, even though we were sinners. Surely, God has gone out of his way for us by giving us life, providing for the maintenance of life, giving us redemption, grace, and many other gifts. He is always the initiator.

LUKE 6:39

"Can a blind person guide a blind person? Will not both fall into a pit?"

MEDITATIONS & LESSONS

✦ Only the Son knows the Father and those to whom the Son has revealed the Father. With regard to knowing the will of God, which all of us should be seeking, we are blind. The human being can know that there is a God and know some basic thoughts of his mind, but even these are difficult to discover, and usually are mixed with error. And since this is the case for all men, it is unwise to accept the teachings of other human beings about God, any more than we accept our own. To know God, we must be taught by him. Otherwise, we are involved in a case of the blind leading the blind.

✦ When we follow the teachings of others about God, rather than what God has revealed about himself, we dwell in ignorance and in error. There is the probability that these teachings will be spiritually damaging to ourselves and to others. Although responsibility can be diminished by ignorance, if one willingly chooses an ignorant or human source to gain knowledge of God's will, rather than the Divine source that is offered in Christ and the Church, one has only himself to blame for errors that ensue. It is quite possible that the pit, into which we may fall, could be hell.

LUKE 6:41

"Why do you notice the splinter in your brother's eye, but do not perceive the wooden beam in your own?"

MEDITATIONS & LESSONS

✦ It is certainly easier to find fault in others than in oneself. It is also much easier to come up with the solution for what is wrong in someone else's life than in our own. It is very difficult to discover what is wrong with ourselves and even more difficult to take action to correct our faults. Yet, we have little tolerance for excuses from others.

✦ We are also much more prone to look for faults in others—so that we can discover even their smallest failings—whereas our own failings many times must be enormous before we pay any attention to them.

LUKE 6:46

"Why do you call me, 'Lord, Lord,' but not do what I command?"

MEDITATIONS & LESSONS

✦ Why do we claim to be religious people and practice sin? Why do we claim to be Catholics and ignore the teaching of the Vicar of Christ? These are impossible questions to answer because they involve a contradiction. We cannot logically do both. The answer should be to choose one or the other. But human beings want to have their cake and eat it too—be "holy" and at the same time enjoy sinful pleasure. But it can not be that way. Christ said that he would vomit the lukewarm out of his mouth.

✦ When we call someone "lord" it implies that that person is our master. In that case, we are obliged to do what the master says. If we are not willing to obey the master, to call him "lord" is a contradiction. This is especially true when the One we call Lord is Jesus.

LUKE 7:24

When the messengers of John had left, Jesus began to speak to the crowds about John. "What did you go out to the desert to see—a reed swayed by the wind?"

MEDITATIONS & LESSONS

✦ It is not an ordinary occurrence for people to travel great distances and suffer great inconvenience, especially when there is little or nothing by way of material reward awaiting them. People can be gripped by hysteria, but it is still well to investigate the phenomenon. There must be some good or attractive aspect to it, from which we can learn.

✦ Truth, the answer to life's mysteries, will still draw people regardless of the times, if properly presented. Even in the best of times, people always have problems in their lives, to which the answers are not readily available. The burden is upon the one who proclaims the Gospel, to do so in an appealing manner—not necessarily a soft manner—but one that will appeal to mind and heart and will inspire action. The truth is not like a reed which bends every time the wind blows.

Luke 7:25

"Then what did you go out to see? Someone dressed in fine garments?"

Meditations & Lessons

✦   Obviously, the people had a very special reason to make a trip into the desert, and they would not have gone in that direction to see a person living in luxury. They would be more likely to find such a person closer to their homes. So they had gone a great distance and experienced some hardship themselves, to see a man who lived a penitential life. Clearly they sensed goodness in this man; they saw him as leading a more ideal life than themselves. Christ is trying to persuade them to adopt some of the Baptist's virtues.

Luke 7:26

"Then what did you go out to see? A prophet?"

Meditations & Lessons

✦   Even the prophet is no one compared to God. The prophet is a "voice in the wilderness" of the world, calling us to serve God.

✦   They went to see a prophet in the sense of a "Savior." Human beings always seem to expect someone else to do the work. If we simply associate ourselves with the person, by some magical means, all will be well without raising a finger to help ourselves, particularly if change will be painful to us.

✦   Usually the basic message is "repent and believe". That is, accept this message from God and live as he wills. If we were already living as God wants us to, there would be no need for a prophet, since the prophet asks us to change. Human beings so oppose basic change in their lives, that they get rid of the prophet—ignore, persecute, or kill him.

LUKE 7:31

"Then to what shall I compare the people of this generation? What are they like?"

MEDITATIONS & LESSONS

✦   People of every generation are alike. In practice, they tend to judge by a subjective rather than an objective standard. Naturally enough, such people often find themselves involved in contradiction. Virtue lies in the middle, but most people are not able to appreciate that balance or live it in their lives. Even when they observe moderation being practiced, as in the life of Christ, two people may interpret that life as being of two different extremes, for example, too strict or too indulgent.

LUKE 7:44

Then he turned to the woman and said to Simon, "Do you see this woman? When I entered your house, you did not give me water for my feet, but she has bathed them with her tears and wiped them with her hair."

MEDITATIONS & LESSONS

✦   For the Pharisee, the answer is "yes and no." He is shocked because he thinks that Jesus does not realize that this woman is a sinner. The Pharisee holds her to be of no account, not worthy of his attention, but Jesus certainly does not see her that way. Whether she may have been unattractive of face, figure, in dress, or due to her unsavory character, the Pharisee was not about to associate with her in any way. For Jesus, she was a person, a creature of God, different from others, perhaps repulsive in some aspects, but deserving of respect and attention as a human being.

✦   "Do you see this woman?" That is, "look at her." It is amazing how likable human beings are, when we come to know them, when we give them a chance to make an unprejudiced impression upon us. Look at what she has done! Look at yourself, what you have done (or have not done). How can you see her as all bad and yourself as all good?

LUKE 8:25

"Where is your faith?"

MEDITATIONS & LESSONS

✦   The lack of faith showed by the Apostles during a storm gave Jesus the opportunity to perform a very powerful miracle. It is true that they lacked faith, but they knew who to turn to in their fear.

✦   The Apostles are like ourselves. Their faith seems strong and vibrant, when everything is going well. When it is tested, we come to see how shallow it can be. The miracles and praise heaped upon Christ made them feel "unbeatable." The storm—and worse, the suffering and death of Christ—saw them despairing. Faith takes great courage!

LUKE 8:30

"What is your name?" He replied, "Legion," because many demons had entered him.

MEDITATIONS & LESSONS

✦ Every single vice is multi-headed. It can appear in a hundred different ways in our lives. Temptation to the same sin comes in many forms, at unsuspected times, in a variety of circumstances. Moreover, where one vice is present, there may well be many. For sin is the result of a weakened will. If the will is undisciplined in one respect, it is likely to be weak in others as well.

LUKE 8:43-45

A woman afflicted with hemorrhages for twelve years, who [had spent her whole livelihood and doctors and] was unable to be cured by anyone, came up behind him and touched the tassel on his cloak. Immediately her bleeding stopped. Jesus then asked, "Who touched me?"

MEDITATIONS & LESSONS

✦ Who was it who touched me with faith? Just as we can often recognize a special note of sincerity or honesty in a person's voice, so

Christ was sensitive to the manner in which he had been touched. It was not someone simply clawing at him to gain attention, but one who truly believed that he had divine power.

   ✦   We can well afford to follow the woman's example. For instance, rather than pushing and shoving to get close to the Pope, maybe we would gain more for ourselves and others by quietly observing his virtues and listening to what he has to say to others. Is this not more likely to affect us spiritually than to have a photograph on the mantel?

LUKE 9:18-20

Once when Jesus was praying in solitude, and the disciples were with him, he asked them, "Who do the crowds say that I am?" They said in reply, "John the Baptist; others, Elijah; still others, 'One of the ancient prophets has arisen.' " Then he said to them, "But who do you say that I am?"

MEDITATIONS & LESSONS

   ✦   The whole context—questions and answers—would seem to give the lie to the claim that Jesus did not know who he was until after the Resurrection. For some mysterious reason, he tried to keep his identity hidden, revealing it only gradually, but that very fact would also indicate that he at least knew who he was.

   ✦   We need to give greater thought to these questions and, with God's grace, develop the same faith conviction as St. Peter. If we don't, our faith will be weak all along the line, and our practice of the faith less than exemplary, and in time of severe temptation, nil. If Christ is God, everything falls into place. If our faith in that fact is weak, everything is "up for grabs".

LUKE 9:25

"What profit is there for one to gain the whole world yet lose or forfeit himself?"

MEDITATION & LESSONS

✦ Almost certainly, the one who operates in this world on selfish principles, at least initially, will profit more than the person who follows God's law in this world. But those "profits" are never secure and are frequently lost. So, even in this world, the worry of insecurity and actual loss are hardly worth the risk of eternal damnation.

✦ "Carrying one's cross", on the other hand, although it does not appear profitable, ordinarily gives to the person a serenity and peace that the wealthy would envy. This comes from putting limitations of various kinds on oneself. It is a knowledge that one is doing God's will, causing no harm and doing much good to one's neighbor, and possessed of a sure hope in God's promises for oneself.

✦ If God is not only charitable, but also just, there must be a day of reckoning, and on that day, the decisions will be obvious; there will be no contention; one has served God or not. It will be a sad day for some, happy for others, but quiet, subdued, in that everyone without exception will know that justice has been done.

LUKE 9:41

"O faithless and perverse generation, how long will I be with you and endure you?"

Meditations & Lessons

✦ So often, human beings only half listen to what is being said. We constantly jump to conclusions and interject our own ideas. Later, we somehow convinced ourselves that the person said what we wanted to hear rather than what he actually said.

✦ A teacher needs patience! People do not learn quickly, but it is not because they lack intelligence. They either do not listen, or they do not think that the message applies to the practical situations in their own lives. A teacher also needs to be repetitive. Sometimes a person hears an idea over and over again without paying it much attention. Later, when the idea comes to his mind, he thinks that it is actually his idea, so he accepts it because it is "his."

Luke 10:15

"And as for you, Capernaum, 'Will you be exalted to heaven?' "

Meditations & Lessons

✦ The implication is that everyone in Capernaum should be exalted to heaven because of the graces received, having the Messiah in their very midst. But for that very reason, a rejection of the Messiah will bring them low.

Luke 10:25-26

There was a scholar of the law who stood up to test him and said, "Teacher, what must I do to inherit eternal life?" Jesus said to him, "What is written in the law? How do you read it?"

MEDITATIONS & LESSONS

✦   Jesus wished to get across that God had already revealed clearly the means of gaining eternal life from the earliest of times (Deut 6:5; Lev 19:18) and that there should be no mystery about that teaching. Everyone should know it, especially one versed in the Law.

✦   The more important question was, "How do you read it?" How do you interpret it? How do you practice it? The response was to the effect that there must be a great deal of subjectivity, arbitrariness in practice because it is difficult to determine who is one's neighbor. Jesus corrected that impression. Everyone, even the poorest, even those considered least worthy of help are neighbors.

✦   It is not that the law is difficult to understand or interpret, but that we wish to justify—to excuse—ourselves from its complete observance. The word "complete" is probably better to use than "strict,"which often implies fundamentalism, scrupulosity, unwillingness to have a certain human flexibility. But notice that flexibility is always in favor of the one exercising it. Jesus asks for the contrary—when in doubt, as the lawyer claims to be, favor the other person.

LUKE 10:36

"Which of these three, in your opinion, was neighbor to the robbers' victim?"

MEDITATIONS & LESSONS

✦   The answer to the question Jesus asks after telling them the parable of the Good Samaritan is obvious. What becomes important is the definition of "neighbor." Neighbor is anyone and everyone in need.

✦   It is not always easy to judge who is truly in need. Actually, the apparently beaten man could be a robber himself who could turn on the Samaritan. It would seem that a person is expected to take that chance.

✦   The Jews understood (see Job), and we, too, often think that the person who is "down on his luck", is in that situation through his own fault because of some "sin" or foolishness of his own doing. This is not necessarily the case, but even if it is, kindness demands that we offer assistance.

✦   Jesus puts aside another mentality—that of justifying oneself; "I need all that I have. I have more than the victim but not enough for both of us." That calculation—what I need and what it will take to help the poor man—usually is very much exaggerated. "My needs" are usually connected with luxury of some kind, at least compared to his desperate need.

Luke 11:11-12

"What father among you would hand his son a snake when he asks for a fish? Or hand him a scorpion when he asks for an egg?"

Meditations & Lessons

✦   In a human relationship, where there is love and dependency, the stronger person is never going to deliberately harm the loved one. He may not be able to respond or he may judge that it is not good to respond to the request, but he will not harm the one making the request. On the other hand, God, we are told, always responds and in a helpful manner.

LUKE 11:13

"If you then, who are wicked, know how to give good gifts to your children, how much more will the Father in heaven give the Holy Spirit to those who ask him?"

MEDITATIONS & LESSONS

✦ We cannot judge God in terms of our selves; nor does our love compare to his love. His gifts are even better than what we ask for.

✦ The Holy Spirit is a wonderful gift from the Father.

✦ The Father answers our prayers.

LUKE 11:18

"And if Satan is divided against himself, how will his kingdom stand?"

MEDITATIONS & LESSONS

✦ For Satan to perform good works would be a total contradiction. It would be a denial of his person and undermine his influence in the world, eventually eliminating him. So Christ, who was clearly performing wondrous good works, cannot be Satan. If not Satan, who is Christ? The works are so wondrous that they must be attributed to some all-powerful Spirit; God is the only alternative answer.

LUKE 11:19

"If I, then, drive out demons by Beelzebul, by whom do your own people drive them out?"

MEDITATIONS & LESSONS

✦   'What is good for the goose is good for the gander.' If Beelzebul is the real power behind the casting out of demons, then he must also be the power used by those who the Pharisees favor. Obviously, the Pharisees were not ready to say that their own people are under the spell of Satan. Thus Jesus silenced them again.

LUKE 11:40

"Did not the maker of the outside also make the inside?"

MEDITATIONS & LESSONS

✦   The Pharisees—and all of us—should be at least as concerned for their internal purity as for their external purity. They may have been perfectly proper in their external appearance and decorum, but inside they were filled with dead men's bones; whitened sepulchers.

✦   Interior purity is even more important than external purity because it is from within—from the mind and heart—that one's conduct is truly determined. Indeed, one may be rich or poor, tall or short, fat or thin but those characteristics make no difference. The poor person can be better than the rich person, the short person better than the tall. The merit of their actions is defined by the quality of their intellect and will.

LUKE 12:6

"Are not five sparrows sold for two small coins?"

MEDITATIONS & LESSONS

✦   Although sparrows are sold cheaply, they have been created by the Lord and provided for. Their lives may seem to be worth nothing to men, but surely God loves and values them. Human life may occasionally be taken cheaply, too, but we are much more valuable than sparrows, and God knows us, loves us, and desires to have our immortal souls for his glory. So we should not care what men do to us as long as our relationship with God is what is should be.

LUKE 12:13-14

Someone in the crowd said to him, "Teacher, tell my brother to share the inheritance with me." [Jesus] replied to him, "Friend, who appointed me as your judge and arbitrator?"

MEDITATIONS & LESSONS

✦   "Consider the lilies of the field, the birds of the air." The goods of this world are not that important. All that we need are the necessities; more than that may distract us from God and get us into trouble.

✦   We can obsess about what we own or what we want, but as Jesus tells us, we may store up earthly treasure but not be rich in what matters to God.

✦   The mission of Christ, the mission of the Church is not to settle worldly disputes, although we propose the principles on which they should be decided. But the actual judgment is the business of politics, understood in a very wholesome sense but in no way to be confused with the practice of religion. The Father did not send Christ to settle worldly disputes.

+ The Lord allows the accumulation of riches in the hands of some, while others are poor. But we have the assurance that in the final analysis God will set things straight.

Luke 12:25-26

"Can any of you by worrying add even a moment to your life-span? If even the smallest things are beyond your control, why are you anxious about the rest?"

Meditations & Lessons

+ It seems that we often worry more about the impossible than we worry about what is under our control and what we are obliged and responsible to do. We should be resigned, accepting, of those things which we cannot change; appreciate that God has his purpose.

+ God loves us. He will care for us. If he has made nature so beautiful and kept it that way by his providence, he is ready to do even more for us.

+ As we contemplate the beauty of nature, which seems far more beautiful than we are, not only exteriorly but interiorly as well, we have reason to understand what damage has been caused by Original Sin and personal sin. We are the crowning point of creation, made in God's own image and likeness and yet we admire so many things in nature as being more beautiful than we are. Why? Sin, abuse of free will, would seem to be the only adequate answer.

Luke 12:28

"If God so clothes the grass in the field that grows today and is

thrown into the oven tomorrow, will he not much more provide for you, O you of little faith?"

MEDITATIONS & LESSONS

✦ Worry is in opposition to faith. When we worry, we are doubting God's providence. If we trust God, we have nothing to worry about.

LUKE 12:42

"Who, then, is the faithful and prudent steward whom the master will put in charge of his servants to distribute [the] food allowance at the proper time?"

MEDITATIONS & LESSONS

✦ Fidelity and perseverance in fidelity are essential. This seems to be the means for most to be saved. Great actions are few and far between, and if there is no continuity, these acts hardly indicate great love and devotion. Daily, unrelenting dedication to one's ordinary responsibilities is much more appreciated.

✦ As in so many other places in the Gospel, love of God is not proven in a direct manner. It is easy to say that one loves God and to "feel" that way, but the real proof is love of one's neighbor. In the parable, the good servant is just and charitable to those around him.

✦ The more responsibility that is given to a person, the more is demanded of that person, the more that person must serve all the rest. This is easy to see in the life of a bishop, but it is true of most any people, including people in business. As one climbs "higher" in responsibility, success depends upon the manner in which one treats others. The purpose of the office is to help others—whether Church or business—and if we are to help others, service is demanded. Many do not understand or appreciate this. It is a difficult burden for the person in authority to bear, when others do not appreciate his task; but there are dreadful results when the person in authority himself does not understand his responsibility.

LUKE 12:51

"Do you think that I have come to establish peace on the earth?"

MEDITATIONS & LESSONS

✦   The obvious answer to the question is "yes." Peace was announced at Christ's birth, and it was an important part of Christ's message. In this statement, he is making the point that each individual person is responsible to God for his actions. Some will accept him; some will deny him. So we should not follow the crowd, not even our family members perhaps, if we wish to be saved.

✦   The Word of God is like a sharp sword that divides people one against the other, depending upon our acceptance or rejection of it. Of course, that same Word of God is intended to be the great unifier (Last Supper). But all depends upon the free will of man. Peace which denies the Word of God is no peace at all.

LUKE 12:56

"You know how to interpret the appearance of the earth and the sky; why do you not know how to interpret the present time?"

Meditations & Lessons

✦   Especially with the preaching of Christ to call them to their senses, the Pharisees should have been able to see the inconsistencies in their practice of the law as compared to God's law of love, goodness, mercy and forgiveness. The Pharisees were weighed down by their own ideas of justice. This meant that they had comparatively little love, goodness, forgiveness, and mercy. Their knowledge of the prophecies concerning the Messiah were a stumbling block to them rather than an aid.

✦   In our own day, we have unlocked many mysteries of nature. Yet, ironically, we do not seem to have enough insight to notice that we have ignored God's moral law. This is leading us deeper and deeper into a quagmire of immorality, in which our own technological genius will be used against us, against all humanity.

✦   We do know how to interpret the present time but are unwilling to do so. We are distracted by pleasure and "progress," but we are unwilling to control them. We lack the good sense and the good will to curb our self-seeking appetites. Therefore we lose the ability to enjoy creation with moderation and to share its benefits with others.

Luke 12:57

"Why do you not judge for yourselves what is right?"

Meditations & Lessons

✦   If we tried to be more objective and less selfish, if we were more ready to forgive, if we were more ready to sacrifice our rights in charity for the cause of peace, we would be a lot better off. It is neither necessary nor profitable to contest every little perceived injustice.

✦　If we are honest with ourselves, we usually can tell what is right and what is wrong and whether we are in the right or in the wrong.

✦　The final judge of these matters, after all, is God. Success is meaningless if we oppress the poor, lack charity, and make unreasonable demands upon God and others. We should look to God's standard of justice, which is colored by compassion, goodness, and love. He looks not only to the matter in question, but also to the condition of the persons involved.

Luke 13:2:4

"Do you think that because these Galileans suffered in this way they were greater sinners than all other Galileans?...Or those eighteen people who were killed when the tower at Siloam fell on them—do you think they were more guilty than everyone else who lived in Jerusalem?"

Meditations & Lessons

✦　How a person dies (cancer, auto accident) regardless of its horror or violence in our eyes, says nothing about the kind of life the person led. Some of the martyrs and other apparently innocent, holy people have suffered greatly.

✦　The seeming unexpectedness of death is not an indication either of injustice on God's part or evil on that of the person. As the subsequent verses indicate, all of us are given countless opportunities—after each sin — to reform our lives through the Sacrament of Reconciliation. None of us can complain when our opportunities for reforming our lives come to an end.

LUKE 13:16

"This daughter of Abraham, whom Satan has bound for eighteen years now, ought she not to have been set free on the sabbath day from this bondage?"

MEDITATIONS & LESSONS

✦ Many people still seem to be more solicitous for their dogs and cats than for their fellow human beings. And if not for dogs and cats, they are more solicitous for material possessions than for unfortunate human beings. It is a sad commentary. Granted that much of what we give to persons in charity is "wasted" in the sense that it does not produce any lasting good, is not the same thing true of providing for an animal, or spending money on things that wear out or are quickly consumed? The only difference is that what we spend on material possessions or on animals is for our pleasure. What we do for people is to please God!

✦ The sabbath is for man, not man for the sabbath. Doing good works does not excuse from any of the sabbath obligations, but when we can fulfill both duties, our course of action should be obvious. We are certainly allowed to do on the day of rest what is necessary to sustain our bodily life. Why should we not be allowed to do what gives life to the soul of the donor and necessary physical assistance to the recipient?

LUKE 13:18

"What is the kingdom of God like? To what can I compare it?"

Meditations & Lessons

✦ The Kingdom of God is absolute simplicity (a mustard seed) and absolute immensity (a large bush). Heaven is not complicated. It is not for rocket scientists only; it is just one thought, one picture for the imagination—God. But the knowledge of God will fill our minds to overflowing and give us unlimited joy, satisfaction, fulfillment.

✦ Our part in bringing about the Kingdom of God, even in our own lives, is very small. God gives us the seed, waters it, nurtures it, and so on. All we need to do is receive the seed (not reject it by a sinful life) and provide fertile soil (virtue) which will help the process along.

✦ The Kingdom of God involves a complete transformation of the person. Even as the seed is nothing like the tree, nor the yeast like the loaf of bread, so we, though children of God now, have no idea what we are going to be like. "What eye has not seen, and ear has not heard, and what has not entered the human heart, what God has prepared for those who love him (1 Corinthians 2:9)."

Luke 14:3-6

"Is it lawful to cure on the sabbath or not?" But they kept silent; so he took the man and, after he had healed him, dismissed him. Then he said to them, "Who among you, if your son or ox falls into a cistern, would not immediately pull him out on the sabbath day?"

Meditations & Lessons

✦ The Commandment is to keep holy the sabbath day. But holiness would seem to consist in loving God with one's whole heart and soul, and loving one's neighbor for love of God. Undoubtedly, the intentions of the rabbis were good, namely, to restrict activity in favor of worshiping God. But Christ pointed out that the second of the two great Commandments was also important for holiness, and nothing should interfere with a good action, especially one which shows concern for both creature and Creator. If one can care for animals because of their value to that person, one can surely care for a fellow human being.

LUKE 14:28,31

"Which of you wishing to construct a tower does not first sit down and calculate the cost to see if there is enough for its completion? ...Or what king marching into battle would not first sit down and decide whether with ten thousand troops he can successfully oppose another king advancing upon him with twenty thousand troops?"

MEDITATIONS & LESSONS

✦   If heaven is truly our goal, we should consider frequently whether or not we are on the right road. And if not, we need to take the logical steps to get back on track and stay there. Otherwise, like the wise steward, we should set our sights on some other goal and pursue that one.

✦   It is obvious that in both the case of the tower and that of war, sacrifices are necessary to attain the goal. For example, in our spiritual life, we need to sacrifice many other, very pleasurable goals to concentrate on the one precious objective. We need to put aside many harmless or indifferent distractions as well. And we need to sacrifice some very legitimate goods simply to strengthen the resolve of our wills.

✦   We very much need the help of others in attaining life's goals, even the goal of eternal life. When we estimate the possibilities of doing something, almost inevitably we find this to be true. When we see that we cannot make it alone, we need the humility to seek the necessary help. This is not always easy.

LUKE 14:34

"Salt is good, but if salt itself loses its taste, with what can its flavor be restored?"

MEDITATIONS & LESSONS

✦   The world may be in a dreadful state, but the situation is never hopeless while there are good people in the world ready to pay the price for virtue. As long as we have these holy people, there is hope. Without them our condition is desperate.

✦   Regardless of how sinful or unworthy a person may feel, despair is the only evil that can kill the person spiritually. As long as we have that spark of desire to be holy, we can catch on fire spiritually once again. When we lose that spark, our cause is desperate indeed.

✦   The basics of the spiritual life—faith, hope, love—are most important. The regular practice of the spiritual exercises can never be abandoned, even at times of great dryness.

LUKE 15:4:8

"What man among you having a hundred sheep and losing one of them would not leave the ninety-nine in the desert and go after the lost one until he finds it?...Or what woman having ten coins

and losing one would not light a lamp and sweep the house, searching carefully until she finds it?"

MEDITATIONS & LESSONS

✦ All of the sheep and all of us are valuable. It is not just one particular sheep for which the shepherd would search. He would look for any or all of the sheep who might be in trouble. His concern is universal.

✦ The whole parable reminds one of the altar boy picnic. Invariably, at the end of the day, when a head count is taken, at least one boy is missing. Are the others less loved by the priest because he goes in search of the lost boy? Hardly; just the opposite.

✦ The mercy, love, compassion, goodness of God is unlimited. The examples that Jesus gives show just how concerned God is for the lost. The shepherd goes into the desert, and the woman sweeps with diligence and does not stop until she has found the coin.

✦ We should not be envious of the concern which the Lord shows for the lost, thinking that "it's good enough for them". The lost sheep could be one of us the next day. We never know when we shall be in need of help. To scorn another or to be envious of him is to be filled with pride.

✦ The Lord never gives up seeking the lost—until he finds it. This reminds us of the poem, *The Hound of Heaven* by Francis Thompson. God is relentless in seeking the sinner. So we remain lost only as long as we will to be lost. If we want to be rescued, and if we look for help, it will be there.

✦ Jesus uses the story of the Prodigal Son to illustrate that when the lost are found they are treated with love and mercy. (Luke 15:11-32).

Luke 16:11

"If, therefore, you are not trustworthy with dishonest wealth, who will trust you with true wealth?"

Meditations & Lessons

   ✦   If one cannot handle his material possessions prudently and honestly, it is unlikely that he or she can be trusted to make sound spiritual judgments. After all, material things can be seen, measured, weighed, and compared precisely with others. Weighing spiritual matters requires a higher degree or prudence as well as discernment, patience, knowledge, wisdom and, of course, honesty.

   ✦   Judgments concerning the things of this world are based on easily perceived motives of self-interest and self-preservation. Our spiritual motivation is based on God's promise, which at times can seem ephemeral, far off, and uncertain. So if self-interest and self-preservation do not lead the individual to make sound judgments in worldly matters, it is unlikely that he or she will be persuaded to make sound judgments for the benefit of the soul, especially when the motivating force seems to be less strong or less immediate.

Luke 16:12

"If you are not trustworthy with what belongs to another, who will give you what is yours?"

Meditations & Lessons

   ✦   At first reading, this question does not seem to make sense because a person is more likely to take better care of his own property than that of another. However, the issue is whether a worker will be given the responsibility compatible with his or her position. For example, if a man works for a company for a certain number of years and is eligible to be promoted to foreman, he will not receive that promotion if he is not deemed to be trustworthy. In this case, it may well be that Jesus is talking about the gifts we receive from the Father. If we are not trustworthy, how can the Father bestow on us the spiritual gifts that he wants us to have?

✦ It is the same with the spiritual life. If we cannot handle our job of giving praise to God in this world, there would be no point in God entrusting that task to us for all eternity. It would be a total waste and absolute foolishness on his part.

LUKE 17:7,9

"Who among you would say to your servant who has just come in from plowing or tending sheep in the field, 'Come here immediately and take your place at table'?... Is he grateful to that servant because he did what was commanded?"

MEDITATIONS & LESSONS

✦ The status between servant and master is never changed. The relationship always remains the same as long as they have their respective roles. One commands; the other obeys. The fact that the servant obeys does not necessarily merit any kind of reward.

✦ Of course, human relationships can change. For example, the servant could be given his freedom. But the relationship between God and man will never change. He is Creator; we are creature. We are promised a reward for our obedience, but as creatures, that obedience is to be expected. It is an unmerited reward because no matter what we do, we could never earn a right to it; our right comes only from God's decision to reward us. So it is also, that if a good servant (or we) finally break the traces and rebel, although the master might have mercy, punishment is justified regardless of our previous good service because we have only been doing what we are expected to do.

✦   Despite the point of these verses, God does, as a matter of fact, treat us far more generously than a master treats his servants.

LUKE 17:17-18

"Ten were cleansed, were they not? Where are the other nine? Has none but this foreigner returned to give thanks to God?"

MEDITATIONS & LESSONS

✦   Giving thanks to God or saying 'thank you' to a fellow creature should be second nature for us because we are so totally dependent, not only on God but also upon one another. We should thank others for what they do for us, but we should also thank God for what others do for us as well, because these "others" are God's creatures. They, like everything else in the world that provides for us, come from God.

✦   Lack of thanksgiving is usually a matter of thoughtlessness. We lose sight of what others have done for us in our excitement and good fortune. But surely, even if one does not give thanks immediately, under normal circumstances we have inner promptings to give thanks later on. If we do not feel these, it is probably due to pride and great selfishness. If we feel prompted to give thanks but we reject that idea, we are well on the path to a prideful and selfish existence.

LUKE 18:2-7

"There was a judge in a certain town who neither feared God nor respected any human being. And a widow in that town used to come to him and say, 'Render a just decision for me against my adversary.' For a long time the judge was unwilling, but eventually he thought, 'While it is true that I neither fear God nor respect any human being, because this widow keeps bothering me I shall deliver a just decision for her lest she finally come and strike me.' " The Lord said, "Pay attention to what the dishonest judge says. Will not God then secure the rights of his chosen ones who call out to him day and night? Will he be slow to answer them?"

MEDITATIONS & LESSONS

✦   If a man who has no regard for God or man will take action if somebody keeps after him, surely God, whose love for man knows no limits, will respond to one who prays to him, even if that person is far less persistent than the widow. The Lord will answer much more quickly and favorably.

✦   The verse speaks of God's "elect." Whether that is applied to his priests or to all the baptized, he will respond even more quickly and favorably to them than to others whom he loves.

✦   We fail to realize who we are in God's sight. We do not understand what a special relationship he has established with us. As a result, we do not appeal to him as we should. We simply do not trust in God and his promises as we should. We put our trust in human leaders, weapons, power, and prestige instead of putting our trust in the One who really loves us.

LUKE 18:8

"But when the Son of Man comes, will he find faith on earth?"

MEDITATIONS & LESSONS

✦   Certainly when Jesus came the first time, he found the people, especially the leaders, lacking in faith. If he came today, it is not likely that he would find much more faith among us. Faith gives us the knowledge that everything valuable comes from God. Only God can give life; he alone has the grace that makes us holy. True love among human beings is impossible without holiness. We stand in constant need of conversion.

LUKE 18:19

"Why do you call me good? No one is good but God alone."

MEDITATIONS & LESSONS

✦   The only reason why we call a person good is that the things which he says and does reflect goodness; they transcend the ordinary mode of human activity which is always tinged with a bit of selfishness. Goodness is a cut above the ordinary and usually requires self-sacrifice.

✦   So much for those who do not believe in God. For believers, of course, goodness means God-likeness. The believer sees goodness as a supernatural virtue, something that comes from God, by his grace, and something which is motivated by him. So goodness is not simply something exceptional in man; it differs not only in degree but in essence. Goodness has a divine quality. Since God has revealed himself, shown us what goodness in the world is (Christ), we have a perfect standard by which we can take our own measure, and from which we can have certainty regarding our virtue or lack of virtue.

+ It is quite basic. If we wish to be good we must keep the Commandments. Granted they are phrased negatively, but they are still the foundation of a life of virtue. We cannot build a life of virtue without obedience to the Commandments. The reason is clear. Violating the Commandments indicates the presence of selfishness; observance of the Commandments turns us to love of God and love of neighbor for love of God.

LUKE 18:41

"What do you want me to do for you?"

MEDITATIONS & LESSONS

+ Spiritually we are all blind. All of us should be pleading for God's mercy that we may "see" and understand his truth so clearly that our faith may be strong and pure, a bulwark against temptation of every kind.

+ The attitude of the blind man stands out in stark contrast to that of the Apostles. They ask, "What are you going to do for us?" as if they had truly earned a reward. The blind man simply begs for mercy. The scene reminds one of the Pharisee and the poor man praying in the Temple. Christ could have been exasperated with the Apostles by this time, but he answers them kindly. It was a joy for him, however, to respond to the blind man.

LUKE 20:4

"Tell me, was John's baptism of heavenly or of human origin?"

MEDITATIONS & LESSONS

✦   Today, we might substitute the Holy Father for John the Baptist. Is his authority from heaven or from men? Like the Pharisees, many theologians might hesitate to answer that question today. If his authority is from heaven, we must obey him; if from men, we have destroyed the Church; we become nothing more than a World Council of Churches. Many Protestants are more accepting of the Pope and long for such a unifier as he, while many Catholics seem intent on destroying him.

✦   All kinds of theological distinctions and hair splitting could be made about John's baptism. But it should be clear that his mission was from heaven. The same is true with the Holy Father. We can discuss the matter of infallibility and other types of papal authority all we want, but we must always come back to the question, "Is his authority from heaven or from men?" And then we must act accordingly.

LUKE 20:41

"How do they claim that the Messiah is the Son of David?"

MEDITATIONS / LESSONS:

✦   The Jews would have difficulty with such a question. That is understandable. The answer has to do with the mystery of God-become-man. Jesus was trying to open their eyes to that possibility, namely, that he who looked like a man was indeed God, Christ, the Messiah, as well. Only a God-man could truly be called Lord and son of David at the same time.

✦   We, too, find the mystery of the Hypostatic Union—the one personality of Christ in which his two natures, God and man, are combined—a difficulty. Great faith is needed for acceptance. Yet, if the testimony of Scripture be true—and certainly it has been tested enough—it is clear that Jesus is both God and man. It is not for us to reason how or why, but only to believe.

LUKE 22:27

"For who is greater: the one seated at table or the one who serves? Is it not the one seated at table?"

MEDITATIONS & LESSONS

✦   The Apostles had been arguing about which one of them was the greatest. Jesus continues to try to make the Apostles understand that his Kingdom is not of this world and not like the kingdoms of this world. Obviously, the master is greater than the servant in every worldly sense. Yet Jesus tells the Apostles that he is the One who serves. We should not judge greatness by the standards of the world.

✦   If the Apostles took a good look at themselves, they would see that they were nothing apart from Christ. So why were they arguing? And if they wish to be fully one with Christ, they must live as he lives— lives of humility and without pride—not seeking rewards in this life but in the next.

LUKE 22:35

"When I sent you forth without a money bag or a sack or sandals, were you in need of anything?" "No, nothing," they replied.

MEDITATIONS & LESSONS

✦   We need this same spirit of poverty, this same spirit of dependence. God is good and surely there are great numbers of good people through whom he can and will exercise his mercy. It is not as if we are expecting miracles, that something will come down from heaven as the manna did. But working through natural causes, there is no reason why God cannot provide for us. In fact, he does so in abundance as the support of priests and religious indicates.

✦   Even if we lack something of a material nature, it is clear that we will have more than enough to make up for it in a spiritual sense, and surely the latter is more important. This is the best way to show people the value of the spiritual in comparison to the material.

✦   There is some similarity—but a tremendous difference in degree —in that I depend on the diocese for room (sack), board (money bag), and travel (sandals). But it does not require much faith on my part to believe that these things will be available to me.

LUKE 22:46

"Why are you sleeping?"

MEDITATIONS & LESSONS

✦   The Apostles were probably sleeping because they saw no immediate danger. They were also exhausted psychologically. Jesus was winning every battle of words with the scribes and Pharisees, but he was likely to lose the war because they had the political, worldly power.

✦   When Jesus was going through terrible agony, his disciples, whom he had asked to pray, fell asleep. No matter how tired we are, we always seem to become bright and alert when something important is happening that concerns us. Apparently Christ was trying to make the Apostles more concerned. Although they might not have had anything to fear personally, they should have been more concerned for him.

Luke 22:48

"Judas, are you betraying the Son of Man with a kiss?"

Meditations & Lessons

✦ Yes, he was. And so a kiss, which is a sign of love, was used as an instrument of betrayal. There is something totally illogical about that, even as we sin, we wish to be virtuous or at least to have it appear to others that we are virtuous. We practice virtue with a "halfway" attitude, and many times we commit sin the same way. This attitude is all due to a lack of commitment, which is due to a lack of thought—we lack the conscious awareness of who we are in relation to God and in relation to what he has called us to be.

✦ Every one of our sins is a betrayal, too. Even though there may be mitigating causes that reduce responsibility, when we sin, we still betray the Lord. Many times the underlying cause of our betrayal is our failure to pray. Not merely to petition God, but to raise our hearts and minds to him in a spirit of friendship. Because of this, we stubbornly flirt with the occasions of sin. Very few can resist temptation, if they have not been struggling to reform their lives and be converted to God.

✦ We are great compromisers; we want to have the best of both worlds. And we try to ignore what the Lord said about that. "You are either for me or against me. You cannot serve both God and mammon. The lukewarm I will vomit out of my mouth."

Luke 22:52

"Have you come out as against a robber, with swords and clubs?"

Meditations & Lessons

✦　　The time and the method of Jesus' arrest say a lot about his foes. Far from stealing anything, Christ had given to the people everything that he had received from the Father, and soon would give them his very life on the cross. Certainly they did not need swords and clubs against the Prince of Peace.

✦　　Christ was "robbing" the Pharisees of their power. They were losing their ability to dominate the people because Jesus was revealing the truth to them. In the face of truth, the Pharisees had nothing with which to reply except force, material might. It was not the threat of violence from Jesus but the evil in their hearts that caused them to come against him with swords and clubs.

✦　　Christ refused to let the Apostles respond in kind. He had not come to deliver a message of strict justice (an eye for an eye) or of violence, but a message which transcends these, a message of love and peace.

Luke 23:31

"For if these things are done when the wood is green what will happen when it is dry?"

Meditations & Lessons

✦　　Jesus asked this question as he was carrying his cross on the way to being crucified. The question may be interpreted in different ways, but surely one understanding refers to the presence of Christ being the green wood. If the people cannot appreciate the Messiah when they have him right in their midst preaching, teaching, prophesying, performing miracles, but instead they execute him, how much further will they fall away from the truth at a later date?

LUKE 24:17

"What are you discussing as you walk along?"

MEDITATIONS & LESSONS

✦ Jesus, unrecognized after his Resurrection, asks this question when he joins two disciples on the road to Emmaus. The Disciples were obviously deep in conversation; and when Jesus began to speak to them, they stopped walking, and they were downcast. Their words betrayed their frustration and despair. It is rather obvious that God had no part in what they were doing because they had lost hope. Listening would have been more appropriate and helpful to them. As Jesus suggested immediately (Oh how foolish you are! How slow to believe all the prophets spoke!), they might at least have had the presence of mind to reflect on Scripture, but they did not. They were looking to one another, not to God, not praying. It was the blind leading the blind.

LUKE 24:18-19

"Are you the only visitor to Jerusalem who does not know of the things that have taken place there in these days?" And [Jesus] replied to them, "What sort of things?"

Meditations & Lessons

✦   All the Disciples could think about was the death of Christ. They had forgotten about his miracles and his prophecies. In their despair, they had forgotten about all the good things he had taught them. They had witnessed the mysterious darkness at his death and the dead rising from the tombs. They had heard the words to the good thief and the words of the centurion. They even knew that his tomb had been found empty.

✦   When we despair, it is because we have lost our focus and forgotten God's love and power in our lives.

Luke 24:26

"Was it not necessary that the Messiah should suffer these things and enter into his glory?"

Meditations & Lessons

✦   Theologically, it was not necessary for Christ to undergo all the suffering that he endured. Little more than the Incarnation was necessary. Being of infinite value, even the smallest action of the Son of God would be sufficient.

✦   It was the Father's will which made the suffering necessary. He wished to show, beyond the shadow of a doubt, God's love for man. He did so by asking his son to suffer and die for us. "Greater love than this no man has that a man lay down his life for his friends."

Luke 24:38

"Why are you troubled? And why do questions arise in your hearts?"

MEDITATIONS & LESSONS

✦   The Apostles had reason to be troubled. They had abandoned Christ at Gethsemane; one of their number had betrayed him (Judas); another denied him three times (Peter); and the rest knew that they were no better. Now the Lord has risen; what will he say?

✦   The Apostles had questions and were also troubled because the idea of resurrection from the dead was beyond their comprehension. Even the raising of Lazarus had not sufficiently prepared them to grasp this notion.

✦   They may have been wondering, too, as to what happens now. A few days earlier they had hoped that Christ would lead them to a triumph of some kind. Their hopes were dashed. Now it was necessary to reassess everything, to look at his words and deeds in a different light, to reinterpret them as Christ had meant them. What would this mean for them? It was clear that they would be called upon to do what Christ had done. But how could they, when they were so weak, so powerless?

✦   Experience would prove to the Apostles that God would give them whatever they needed to answer his call and to do his will. He will do the same for us.

LUKE 24:41

"Have you anything here to eat?"

MEDITATIONS & LESSONS

✦   Some of the Apostles' questions must have concerned whether Jesus had been changed by the Resurrection. Eating was a good answer to that question. But was this person the same Jesus, whom they knew?

The gospel of repentance for the forgiveness of sins (verse 47) certainly answered that. There was nothing miraculous about the ordinary way in which Christ conducted his life; he was fully human. There was nothing human about the manner in which he rose from the dead; he is fully God.

CHAPTER FOUR

Questions Jesus Asked in the Gospel of John

J ohn, the beloved disciple, was a magnificent writer who was able to convey the mystery and the majesty of the Christ in a very powerful way. Whether he is recounting the conversation Jesus had with Nicodemus in the garden or his revelation to the woman at the well that he is the Messiah or his declaration on being the bread of life or revealing to the Disciples the coming of the Holy Spirit, one is filled with awe.

JOHN 1:36-38

As he [John the Baptist] watched Jesus walk by, he said, "Behold, the Lamb of God." The two disciples heard what he said and followed Jesus. Jesus turned and saw them following him and said to them, "What are you looking for?"

Meditations & Lessons

✦   Jesus does not ask questions out of idle curiosity or to just make conversation. So his question is really asking for what their souls are searching.

✦   These men were disciples of John the Baptist whose role was:

a) To make straight the way of the Lord.

b) To decrease so that he might increase.

c) To live a penitential way of life.

d) To proclaim the Lamb of God who would take away the sins of the world.

So we might expect that followers of John would be searching for the same person, the Messiah, as they indeed were.

✦   This incident indicates that the two men, who were destined to be Apostles, saw that John the Baptist's way of life was transitional. They seemed to expect that the Messiah's role was different. The Messiah was to lead his people to glory. Jesus knew their thoughts, but he could also see good faith and other qualities in them that indicated that they were the ones chosen by the Father as his Apostles. In vocation, we look for what the Father wants, not what we judge to be "perfect" from a human standpoint.

✦   If we address the Lord's questions to ourselves, we must decide whether we are seeking riches, prestige, and worldly power, or the Way, the Life, and the Truth.

John 1:48-50

Nathanael said to him, "How do you know me?" Jesus answered and said to him, "Before Philip called you, I saw you under the fig tree." Nathanael answered him, "Rabbi, you are the Son of God; you are the King of Israel." Jesus answered and said to him, "Do you believe because I told you that I saw you under the fig tree?"

Meditations & Lessons

✦ Strangely, "natural" wonders often seem more impressive to us than the supernatural. In a way, we have a means of "proving" that the natural wonder took place and cannot be explained except by a person's extraordinary power. When a supernatural event takes place, it is either of a spiritual nature (the forgiveness of sin) or so unusual (the instant cure of blindness or a fatal disease) that it is beyond the power of any earthly being. Miracles are certainly signs of God's power, but God can work through human beings to achieve remarkable results. There is no way of "proving" that; it takes faith.

✦ Surely the fact that Christ knew where Nathanael was is a sign of exceptional power, but it could be explained by his power of observation (for example, grass or dirt on clothes). If human beings can accept such deeds fairly easily, why cannot we accept true miracles? Again, the answer is faith! Faith is confirmed or "proven" only after we have ruled out all natural explanations and "nothing" is left—nothing except God. But if there is a God, who wishes to speak to us, surely this is the way, the only way, in which he can "prove" to us that it is indeed he speaking.

JOHN 2:3-4

When the wine ran short, the mother of Jesus said to him, "They have no wine." Jesus said to her, "Woman, how does your concern affect me? My hour has not yet come."

MEDITATIONS & LESSONS

✦   This verse puzzles us a bit, of course, because it reveals so much of the humanity of Jesus. God makes his will known to us most often through human instruments. In this case, Mary is his instrument who prompts Jesus to work his first public miracle.

✦   A wedding feast might not seem the most appropriate occasion for performing his first miracle. It was a semi-private gathering, a convivial and social event. But God may call upon us at times to do his will in circumstances that we feel are inappropriate—at times that may even be embarrassing to ourselves or to others.

✦   The very circumstances which make it seem like a less appropriate time for Christ's first miracle are the very signs that indicate to us God's love for all men and for each individual person. He desires to serve the humble and to be accepted by them as well as by the rich and powerful; he intends to bring salvation in and through the ordinary things of the world; and by his actions, he demonstrates his love for his mother and how she should be honored.

JOHN 3:5-10

Jesus answered and said to him, "Amen, amen, I say to you, no one can enter the kingdom of God without being born of water and Spirit...Do not be amazed that I told you, 'You must be born from above.' "....Nicodemus answered and said to him, "How can this happen?" Jesus answered and said to him, "You are the teacher of Israel and you do not understand this?"

MEDITATIONS & LESSONS

✦ The same problem exists today as in the time of Christ. Our teachers do not seem to understand what God has revealed to us. Christ would probably say as he did then, however, that the reason is not lack of intelligence but hardness of heart.

✦ Nicodemus does what any true theologian should do. He goes to Christ and asks for his answer. We teachers today are too interested in our own opinions. And seeing this, our people decide that, if we cannot agree among ourselves, they, too, are just as well off to follow their own opinions.

✦ There is not so much a need to understand God's revelation— much of it is mysterious—but there is a need to accept his teaching and pass it on unchanged to others. The work of the teacher is to use appropriate words and examples for the people and derive more detailed applications of the truths that God has revealed to us. But we are not to change it one iota.

JOHN 3:12

"If I tell you about earthly things and you do not believe, how will you believe if I tell you about heavenly things?"

MEDITATIONS & LESSONS

✦ If we cannot understand the things that take place in our very selves such as the presence of the Holy Spirit—how can we expect to understand the mysteries that only the mind of God comprehends? Yet, many people, because they cannot comprehend these great mysteries refuse to believe in God or to follow his commands. They follow something that they can understand—their own opinions.

✦ Although it is extremely helpful to study theology, to know more about God, it is far better to have a simple faith. Assure oneself that God has spoken and then accept his word and practice it. This is the example of St. Thomas More and so many other great saints who had the capacity for both. Simple faith was dominant in their lives.

✦ In his time and now, many people find it difficult to know God in Jesus. Yet, it is Jesus who reveals the Father to us and explains our relationship to him. Some seek to know God through nature. Nature reveals the existence of God clearly enough, but it does not explain our relationship to him and how we are to act, nor does it reveal his plan for our salvation. To deliberately turn from God's word in Scripture and the Church is foolish. In many instances, when Church members turn away, it is because they so poorly live the teachings of Scripture and the Church.

JOHN 4:35

"Do you not say, 'In four months the harvest will be here'?"

MEDITATIONS & LESSONS

✦ Experience teaches us the laws of nature. Yet, God created nature, and his knowledge is complete while ours is imperfect. So when he reveals something to us, we should listen.

✦ For followers of Christ, there is never any reason to be waiting around, looking for something to do. There is always an abundant harvest waiting for the workers to get busy on. Dynamic as Americans are, we also have a tendency to be constantly counting numbers, assessing resources, making great plans to do great things, and we use up a lot of time that could have been used in doing the job.

John 5:2-6

Now there is in Jerusalem at the Sheep [Gate] a pool called in Hebrew Bethesda, with five porticoes...One man was there who had been ill for thirty-eight years. When Jesus saw him lying there and knew that he had been ill for a long time, he said to him, "Do you want to be well?"

Meditations & Lessons

✦   The man of whom the question is asked blamed his failure to be healed on others. But the Lord asks us the same question. We too can blame others—the world around us—for our failure to be healed. We cannot heal ourselves, but faith in God can heal us. The real question is do we have faith in him. That amounts to the same thing as asking do we really want to be healed. For many, it is a more comfortable position to remain immersed in the ways of the world, in our pain and anxiety and hopelessness, and to blame others for our predicament.

✦   There is no question that we need the help of others in order to be healed spiritually. God is the cause of our healing, but most of the time, he works through natural causes. We should be dependent only on God, but we should look to others as possible sources of his help. However, we should realize that our dependence must ultimately be on God and not on human beings. We should also be ready to help others find God—for then God's grace is working through us.

✦   Will power—truly desiring to be healed—is essential on our part. Without that firm desire, God's grace will do little because he has determined from the beginning to leave us perfectly free.

JOHN 5:44

"How can you believe, when you accept praise from one another and do not seek the praise that comes from the only God?"

MEDITATIONS & LESSONS

✦   In preaching to the people, our main question should be whether or not we are preaching the truth that God wants communicated. Most of the time our main question is, "What do the people need to hear? What are they looking for?" This often leads us to discover what God wants preached. But better still, we should ask ourselves that direct question, "What does God want to say to the people today? How would he say it? What is the unvarnished truth concerning that subject?"

✦   If one of our concerns in preaching is to win the praise of others, we are not likely to preach the unvarnished truth of God in the clear terms he would use. It is only when we have the "glory of God" in mind, that we can speak with faith and full conviction and be received in faith by the people.

JOHN 5:46-47

"For if you had believed Moses, you would have believed me, because he wrote about me. But if you do not believe his writings, how will you believe my words?"

MEDITATIONS & LESSONS

✦ God works through human instruments. Even the Son of God, in order to communicate with man, must use words and other suitable signs. On the surface, there is no difference between the appearance of Moses' words and actions and those of Jesus. However, the difference is in the content. And so, if the people could not believe the words of Moses, hallowed by tradition, and embodying more "reasonable" concepts, it would be difficult to believe the extraordinary concepts that the people were hearing from and seeing in Christ with their own eyes and ears.

JOHN 6:5

When Jesus raised his eyes and saw that a large crowd was coming to him, he said to Philip, "Where can we buy enough food for them to eat?"

MEDITATIONS & LESSONS

✦ Christ had compassion for people, especially people in need, and, in this instance, took responsibility for their welfare.

✦ The real need of the people who flocked to Jesus was spiritual food. And Jesus uses their need as an opportunity to perform a great miracle.

✦ If his chief concern had been on natural food, he could have called attention to the people's hunger earlier (in some narrations, the people are with Jesus for three days). The best answer the Apostles could have given, to show their understanding, is, "What really matters is not food but that you are with us."

✦   It was clearly impossible to buy bread for such a large crowd. Jesus was looking for faith in his ability to provide. But no such faith was expressed. So, he tried again to instill faith by multiplying the loaves and the fishes. But even after witnessing that miracle, the people and many of the Disciples were still not ready to accept who he was.

JOHN 6:61-62

"Does this shock you? What if you were to see the Son of Man ascending to where he was before?"

MEDITATIONS & LESSONS

✦   Jesus had just told the Jews that he is the Bread of Life, and added, "Unless you eat the flesh of the Son of Man and drink his blood, you do not have life within you." Many of those who heard his words, could not accept what they heard. To them, Jesus was talking about cannibalism and/or some sensational magic power, that he could give his flesh and blood to them as food and drink and that he could ascend to the heavens. If he walked our streets and made this declaration today, how many of us would have thought he was insane?

✦   If we were told this today, many would declare the speaker insane. But the Jews believed in a Messiah, one who would be empowered by God to save them from their sins, and therefore, capable of most anything. How was he to prove himself the Messiah unless he made some claims which seemed outlandish and then fulfill them?

✦   Although Jesus' claims were hard to accept, not everyone rejected them. People like Nicodemus and the Apostles question Jesus in order to better understand what he was saying and to overcome their doubts or misgivings. Yet the words Jesus spoke remained mysterious.

✦ In the end, it is a matter of faith. We hear the words of Jesus and witness his works, and we either believe in him and in what he says, or we do not.

John 6:66-67

As a result of this many [of] his disciples returned to their former way of life and no longer accompanied him. Jesus then said to the Twelve, "Do you also want to leave?"

Meditations & Lessons

✦ Jesus was willing "to go it alone", if others would not accept his word. He would rather die than deny, or even soften, the truth of the Father. Eventually he did die—in defense of God's truth and in the face of almost total rejection.

✦ So often the results of one's faithfulness to God after many have turned away are not seen by that person; he dies first. Look at all the saints. That is what it means to live by faith—to do the will of God, even without the approbation of men and sometimes in the face of their opposition.

✦ It is hard to comprehend the magnitude of the gift of freedom that God has given to us with no strings attached. Not only do we have freedom to turn from God's will, but we can even directly oppose it. And still his understanding, compassion, and mercy are shown to us after our sin, every time!

John 6:70

"Did I not choose you twelve? Yet is not one of you a devil?"

MEDITATIONS & LESSONS

✦   Betrayal is a part of the human condition. When it comes to
envy, power or money, we can expect that some people will betray us and
that even in small things some will prove to be disloyal.

✦   In the Church, laziness and indifference is a kind of disloyalty.
How a bishop needs loyal priests and people! It is not those who agree
with him on every issue—or at least seem to—that a bishop needs
because they can be among the most disloyal hypocrites. He needs those
who have faith and respect for the sacramental order of episcopate.

JOHN 7:19

*"Did not Moses give you the law? Yet none of you keeps the law.
Why are you trying to kill me?"*

MEDITATIONS & LESSONS

✦   If we are to sin, we must in a sense kill Jesus—out of our lives.
And so we fall away from our prayer life, from priest associates, from
practices of piety, from the essentials of Mass, Penance, Eucharistic devotion. We cannot really kill Christ, but we can effectively push him out of
our lives.

✦   Why do we do this? The answer is clear. If God is in our lives in
any substantial fashion, we must do his will. We cannot avoid it. If he is
present, he is going to run the show, not because he wills to dominate but
because we will it so. On the other hand, if we will to run things our way,
we cannot do so, if God has a central place in our lives. It is a contradiction. The same old story, we must choose between doing God's will and
our own. We cannot serve God and mammon.

John 7:23

"If a man can receive circumcision on a sabbath so that the law of Moses may not be broken, are you angry with me because I made a whole person well on the sabbath?"

Meditations & Lessons

✦ Either it is all right to help a person on the sabbath, or it is not. One part of the body is not better than another part, nor better than the whole. And as for the strenuousness of the exercise, surely Christ was exerting himself very little in comparison to others. Probably the laws were well intended; Christ's objection is that the Pharisees stressed their man-made laws much more than the divine precepts, especially charity.

✦ Anger and envy seem to have been the controlling passions in the Pharisees opposition to Jesus. The Pharisees could not very well get angry about a miraculous healing. But they could get angry with a person who was putting them to shame. Their major fault in this was that they never gave Christ a chance, never gave serious consideration to his claims. They were totally concerned with themselves rather than with truth and with service of the people.

John 8:10

"Woman, where are they? Has no one condemned you?"

Meditations & Lessons

✦ We are all sinners. Each of us can call to mind something we are ashamed of. The woman Jesus speaks to had been caught in adultery and faced death by stoning. Yet her accusers were also sinners. And when Jesus pointed that out, they dropped their stones and slipped away.

+ The thought of putting someone to death should fill us with shame. For even if we are rather holy, there still is not much difference between one human being and another, certainly not enough to make the "holy" person so vastly superior. So even if sin did not hold us back from casting the first stone, the desire to remain holy would.

+ There is no sin that God cannot or will not forgive. If those who were about to kill the woman relented, how much more merciful will be the God who has created us out of love and cherishes us as a parent loves a child—far more. With God, there is not only lack of condemnation, there is mercy, forgiveness, and love.

JOHN 8:43

"Why do you not understand what I am saying? Because you cannot bear to hear my word."

MEDITATIONS & LESSONS

+ To hear the word of God, that is to receive it, means to change. The people only wanted to be told what they wanted to hear. If we listen with the ears of faith, we should understand what we are called to do.

+ It is difficult to accept preaching that demands a real change. We should be patient with people. Even those who wanted change (I have wanted greater participation of laity since ordination) have difficulty in accepting change because God does not seem to be bringing it about the way we would do it. If he would only do what we tell him!

JOHN 8:46

"Can any of you charge me with sin?"

MEDITATIONS & LESSONS

✦ No one could find any evil in Jesus, even though they very much disagreed with what he said and did. They could not deny the truth of what they could understand; the rest made sense in light of their expectation of a Messiah, but they could not accept in faith "a man like us in all things but sin." They wanted the Messiah but one who would fit their preconceived notions of what a Messiah should be.

JOHN 8:46

"If I am telling the truth, why do you not believe me?"

MEDITATIONS & LESSONS

✦ Jesus answers his own question, "Whoever belongs to God, hears the words of God; for this reason you do not listen, because you do not belong to God (verse 47)." If we are in opposition to God, we do not listen to what he says.

✦ The willingness of Jesus to challenge shows his self-assurance. He knew who he was. It is extremely difficult to say that I am right and everyone else is wrong. It takes more than courage, it takes conviction and faith of an absolute kind.

✦ There is nothing so clear and convincing as the truth. Truth is like a knife going through butter. Nothing—no doubt—can truly resist it. The writings of great scholars show this plainly: St. Thomas, St.

Augustine, St. Thomas More, Cardinal Newman, etc. And yet, the people fought against the truth with their irrational arguments. We do the same, when we sin or when we deliberately do something that is less than the best.

John 10:34-36

"Is it not written in your law, 'I said, "You are gods" '? If it calls them gods to whom the word of God came, and scripture cannot be set aside, can you say that the one whom the Father has consecrated and sent into the world blasphemes because I said, 'I am the Son of God'?"

Meditations & Lessons

✦   We can become godlike by hearing the Word of God, meditating upon it, and putting it into practice. Our works do not make us godlike, but the grace of God within us transforms them to a higher plane.

✦   If God can "divinize" the actions of men—which would appear most difficult—then there should be no problem in believing that God can "humanize" his Son, sending him into the world with a human nature.

✦   Pride leads us to put more credence in our own powers and less in God's power—even though the insufficiency of our own powers is demonstrable. To put credence in God's power demands an act of faith. We can verify our insufficiency scientifically and through experience. We are subject to sickness, death, and other woes, and we cannot really control nature. Who among us can quiet a storm at sea?

John 11:7-9

He said to his disciples, "Let us go back to Judea." The disciples said to him, "Rabbi, the Jews were just trying to stone you, and you want to go back there?" Jesus answered, "Are there not twelve hours in the day?"

Meditations & Lessons

✦ Time is a precious gift of God. Time is opportunity, which we have only once and will never have again. We must take full advantage of what is given to us.

✦ We should not avoid taking action because it might lead to conflict. Keeping the peace is not a sufficient reason to do nothing when we should do something. Our main concern should be to do God's will in a constructive manner.

✦ Jesus was not afraid to go back to Judea, but the Disciples may have been. Sometimes, in order to follow Jesus, we must put aside fear or follow him despite our fear.

John 11:25-26

"I am the resurrection and the life; whoever believes in me, even if he dies, will live, and everyone who lives and believes in me will never die. Do you believe this?"

Meditations & Lessons

✦ This is the only question that God really asks of us. Everything follows from the answer we give. If we believe that there is a God and

Jesus is the Son of God, there are no more questions. We simply do God's will as it has been revealed to us by Christ and in his Church.

✦ We make religion very complicated these days. As if our faith should depend upon the validity of this theological opinion or that, upon this external practice or that! All that really matters is that God, Christ, the Church has said so. Using God's gift of reason, we may do all the speculating and theologizing that we wish to try to strengthen our faith, but in the end, our religion is very simple. Do we believe Jesus or not?

✦ When Jesus asks, "Do you believe?" we sense the complete freedom that he gives to each person. There is no pressure whatsoever. We can sense his love and his anxious desire that we follow him. But he does not force us to believe. He does not even exert moral pressure—except that which exudes from his very being, his words, and his actions. In this decision—to believe or not—we hold the world in our hands. God puts himself at our mercy. We are in the "driver's seat," and he will permit us to stay there. But if we do so, one day we will discover definitely that choosing our own will over that of God's has been a dreadful mistake, ending in utter despair, hopeless unhappiness.

John 11:39-40

Jesus said, "Take away the stone." Martha, the dead man's sister, said to him, "Lord, by now there will be a stench; he has been dead for four days." Jesus said to her, "Did I not tell you that if you believe you will see the glory of God?"

Meditations & Lessons

✦ Faith, to be perfect, must be absolute, completely without doubt or hesitation. The family of Lazarus had great faith, but did not accept death as something that God wills and from which great good can come. Everything that happens is known to God's Providence, and good can be derived even from the evil that is permitted.

◆ We cannot begin to imagine the glory of God. Even the greatest of miracles reveal only a small glimpse of his glory. Perhaps the epiphanies after the Resurrection are the greatest of the manifestations, but even these are limited. "Blessed are those who have not seen, but believe"— and that includes everyone, even the Apostles.

JOHN 12:27

"I am troubled now. Yet what should I say? 'Father, save me from this hour'?"

MEDITATIONS & LESSONS

◆ What should I say, when I am in trouble? I usually ask to be saved from the difficulty rather than to be given the grace to sustain the burden so that the power of God's grace can be made manifest. It is perfectly well to use what human means we have at our disposal (for example, in cases of sickness and unjust attack), but we should never forget the power of prayer. Nor should we ever forget that one way or another even the "evil" that befalls us is ultimately intended for God's honor and glory.

◆ In time of trouble more than any other time, I should place myself in God's hands, at his disposal. When we rely on human efforts, we usually depend heavily on another person. If we depend upon their ability and their sense of justice, how much more should we rely upon the "ability and justice" of God!

John 13:12

"Do you realize what I have done for you?"

✦   What Christ did by washing the feet of the Apostles was to teach them by example the spirit of humility and service that should animate their lives. To serve is to reign. And to serve the lowliest is to reign in the heights, to be closer to Christ.

✦   I should look more for such opportunities to imitate the humility of Jesus; I'm usually in such a hurry that the opportunity has passed before I realize that there was one.

✦   At least this example—undoubtedly there are others—would indicate that there is something to style and image. Washing of the feet was a symbolic gesture used to teach the Apostles. As a bishop, it would be well to look into symbolic ways of teaching. One must be careful not to allow style to replace substance, but outward signs of inner convictions are most necessary in teaching.

John 14:2

"In my Father's house there are many dwelling places. If there were not, would I have told you that I am going to prepare a place for you?"

Meditations & Lessons

✦   Christ appeals to his absolute truthfulness to gain the agreement of the Apostles. He has been so completely honest with them that it would be impossible that he could be deceiving them on anything, no matter what he might say. Would we be able to resort to the same kind of appeal as a proof of our statement?

♦   Union with the Father is the reward for faithfulness to Christ. The metaphor of many mansions is effective in suggesting that there are degrees of glory in Heaven. Certainly in this world, we do not expect to get the choicest rooms, when we go to a hotel. Those are given to the rich and powerful. Similarly, those who are spiritually rich and powerful will experience a greater degree of glory in Heaven (best rooms) than those who have served God, but less well.

John 14:9-10

"Have I been with you for so long a time and you still do not know me, Philip? Whoever has seen me has seen the Father. How can you say, 'Show us the Father'? Do you not believe that I am in the Father and the Father is in me?"

Meditations & Lessons

♦   How long we have known Christ, or rather have had the opportunity to know Christ, and how little we have learned of him. We have had devoted parents, good teachers, priests and sisters, opportunities for study, for prayer, for hearing inspirational speakers, but how little have we made this our own. The cares of the world or our activities, which are good in themselves, frequently take us from prayerful reflection, which is so necessary, if we are to come to know the Lord.

♦   The mystery of the Trinity was not within Philip's frame of reference. Perhaps, to some degree, we are like Philip. But the Trinity calls for much reflection, even though it is a mystery. Since there is only one God, even though the Persons are distinct, wherever one Person is, there are the other two. This is particularly important for an appreciation of the indwelling of the Holy Spirit. Wherever the Spirit is, there are the Father and Son as well.

John 16:29-31

His disciples said, "Now you are talking plainly and not in any figure of speech. Now we realize that you know everything and do not need to have anyone question you. Because of this we believe that you came from God." Jesus answered them, "Do you believe now?"

Meditations & Lessons

✦   Figurative language is the best for explaining that which is a mystery. When Christ stopped using figures of speech and spoke plainly, the Disciples thought that they understood. But faith is required; we will never understand fully. The words Christ used might have been more intelligible in themselves, but without figures for the imagination, they do not signify as much. In a sense, the more we understand about mysteries, the less we understand them.

✦   Theology is "faith seeking understanding". Children first believe what parents and teachers tell them and then gradually come to understand. The same goes for "the children of God". Unless we first believe, we will never understand anything. Our primary desire and boast should not be that we understand, but that we believe.

John 18:4 & 7

"Whom are you looking for?"

MEDITATIONS & LESSONS

✦ Notice with what little importance the Apostles are regarded. It was obvious that even though they may have preached and performed miracles in Jesus' name, they were powerless apart from Jesus. If only we were more consciously aware of the same truth! All our power is from Jesus. "Apart from me, you are nothing."

✦ It would be wonderful if we, who have every motive to seek Jesus, would do so with the zest and energy of those who came out to arrest him! This is the type of reaction he longs for. It is similar to those who pursued Jesus across the lake after the loaves and fishes miracle. Human beings by nature are always seeking someone, something for themselves. If that someone is not Jesus, the devil will certainly fill the vacuum. We will set our hearts on something. Who is our prize?

JOHN 18:11

"Shall I not drink the cup that the Father gave me?"

MEDITATIONS & LESSONS

✦ It is not always necessary to accept stoically every misfortune that comes our way. We are surely allowed to defend ourselves to ward off evil. On the other hand, we are not obliged to use self defense in every instance. If we face disagreeable events that we simply cannot avoid, acceptance of God's will is the best course to follow. Everything happens in God's good providence; accepting our circumstances is accepting what God wills for us.

John 18:21

"Why ask me? Ask those who heard me what I said to them. They know what I said."

Meditations & Lessons

◆   If one testifies in his own behalf, the testimony is of no value unless it is confirmed by others. Many people had heard Jesus teach. In fact, the Pharisees had deliberately trailed him and tried to catch him in his speech. If anyone could convict him, it would be these men. Apparently they could not do so, and those who tried to convict him, contradicted one another. The purpose of the question then was deceitful. It was not designed to discover the truth (which they knew) but to trip Jesus if they could. Many reporters do the same thing today. They know one's position but phrase a question in such a way, so that they may get a compromising or sensational statement.

John 18:23

"If I have spoken wrongly, testify to the wrong; but if I have spoken rightly, why do you strike me?"

Meditations & Lessons

◆   This is a good example of authoritarianism. The reason for striking Jesus was probably that the guard considered him to be an inferior person, and he wanted to emphasize that. The guard may also have wanted to curry favor with the authorities.

✦ There still is a great temptation, when we have made a mistake, to take it out on others, trying to relieve ourselves of the blame, or at least the frustration. Usually this can be done successfully only when the strong are oppressing the weak, but anyone might try it. It is the height of cowardice.

JOHN 18:33-34

So Pilate went back into the praetorium and summoned Jesus and said to him, "Are you the King of the Jews?" Jesus answered, "Do you say this on your own or have others told you about me?"

MEDITATIONS & LESSONS

✦ Right up to the last, Christ made every effort to win all men to his Father. Christ's question seems to be an invitation to Pilate to believe that he was sent from God, since there was no compelling reason for Pilate to ask that question. However, it did become Pilate's reason for ordering Christ's death. Pilate could not convict Christ on the basis of the Jewish charges, but he could do so for insurrection. So although there was no proof of Christ claiming civil power of any kind, Pilate held him guilty of this. For political reasons, he decided that it was best to execute Christ, so he made his decision as judge on those grounds, not on the evidence. Today, in Congress, the abortion debate is fueled by politics and not by reason.

JOHN 20:29

"Have you come to believe because you have seen me?"

Meditations & Lessons

✦   When Thomas was presented with physical evidence (which all the other apostles had received, too, of course), it was not so much a matter of believing as accepting the facts before his eyes. But it was an act of faith to go from the fact of Christ's presence to confessing him as, "My Lord and my God!"

✦   We have so much testimony now over two thousand years concerning Christ that morally it amounts to "physical evidence." We make an act of faith, but it does not have the overwhelming strength and conviction of the Apostles. For their faith drove them to full commitment, a life of total dedication to God, while in so many ways our own faith remains intellectual or lukewarm in action.

John 21:16&17

"Simon, son of John, do you love me?"

Meditations & Lessons

✦   The meaning of this question is wrapped up in the meaning that we attach to the word "love." Surely it calls to mind, "No greater love has any man than to lay down his life for his friends...If you love me, keep my commandments...Love God with your whole mind, heart, soul, strength; love your neighbor as yourself." The question may ask more, but at least the Lord is looking for total dedication to him, which is proven in one's total dedication to his friends—all persons created by God.

✦   The relationship between love of God and love of man is brought out very strongly. If you love me, take care of those who are mine (Feed my lambs, feed my sheep). There has been a tendency to forget this, to give lip service to the principle of loving one's neighbor, or to hold it up as a general ideal for all society. Jesus seems to be speaking of something more immediate, direct, personal, if we can judge by the example of his own life.

JOHN 21:22

"What if I want him to remain until I come? What concern is it of yours?"

MEDITATIONS & LESSONS

+ We can only conjecture as to the exact meaning of this question and the manner in which it was fulfilled. It seems to indicate, as Tradition does, that St. John was not to die a martyr's death, but that the Lord would come for him, when he wished.

+ What is more important is the meaning the question had for Peter. "Even if I have just appointed you my vicar on earth, mind your own business. I am God, not you. As vicar you are to do my will. I will handle some matters directly. But no matter what, understand once and for all the lesson that I have tried to teach you. As to the results of all this—what men do or do not do—that is for God to settle. Your service to God is to declare his will as revealed by me. Your service to men is to carry out God's will in your own life, and by your example and your words, give others encouragement to do the same."

PART TWO

Questions Others Asked in the Gospels

In the Gospels, people ask questions for a variety of reasons. The principal reason for a question, of course, is to acquire information. For example, the Disciples frequently asked Jesus to explain something they did not understand. But sometimes questions are rhetorical and do not require an answer—as when John the Baptist asks the Pharisees, "Who warned you to flee from the coming wrath?"

Sometimes questions are indirect because the person is afraid to ask a direct question or is only ready to receive a partial answer. When Jesus quiets the storm at sea, for example, the Disciples ask, "What sort of man is this, whom even the winds and sea obey?" They could have asked, "Is Jesus the Messiah?" or "How is it that he has such power?" or they could have gone directly to Jesus and asked him those questions.

Some of the questions are meant to trap Jesus. For example, Matthew 22:15-17 recounts how the Pharisees and the Herodians tried to trap

Jesus by asking, "Teacher, we know that you are a truthful man and that you teach the ways of God in accordance with the truth. And you are not concerned with anyone's opinion, for you do not regard a person's status. Tell us, then, what is your opinion: Is it lawful to pay the census tax to Caesar or not?" One has the impression that the foes of Jesus had sat down together and tried to come up with a question that would be impossible for him to answer without getting himself in trouble. But first they decided to try to put him off guard by praising him. If Jesus answered that the Roman tax should not be paid, he would have been judged an insurrectionist, an enemy of the Roman Empire. If he said the tax should be paid, he would, in effect, be saying that it was proper for Israel to be subject to the Romans. If Jesus had tried to avoid answering the question by saying, "I don't know," he would have been scorned.

But his answer was immediate, and it disarmed his enemies. Indeed, his answer indicates how remarkable he was.

By meditating on the questions his foes asked, we become aware of the pressure that Jesus was constantly under and of how dangerous and persistent his enemies were. We also see that his foes were no match for him. At the same time, we see how the questions of his foes are used to defeat them and to add to our knowledge.

As we meditate on this section of Bishop Marshall's writings, it would be good to focus on who is asking the question and why it is being asked. We may also ask why, of all the many events that took place in the life of Jesus, is the evangelist recounting this particular episode and this particular question?

CHAPTER FIVE

Questions Others Asked in the Gospel of Matthew

MATTHEW 2:1-2

When Jesus was born in Bethlehem of Judea, in the days of King Herod, behold, magi from the east arrived in Jerusalem, saying, "Where is the newborn king of the Jews?"

MEDITATIONS & LESSONS

✦   Some Scripture scholars point out that the story of the Magi could be "myth." Even if it is, it still shows that the early Christians saw Jesus as King of the Jews. That, as a title, would mean a great deal to them. Jesus was in the line of David, and the title was convincing evidence that he was the Messiah.

✦   Unlike the magi, we do not need to look far for Jesus today. We know where he is. He is present in the tabernacle, the Mass, and the sacraments. Our problem is that we do not seek him. And when we do seek him, if our assistance at Mass and reception of the sacraments is done out of a sense of obligation, we hardly have the ardor, the devotion of the Magi, who "fell down and worshiped him". We call Jesus our brother, but why don't we fall down (kneel) and worship him in our hearts? Perhaps, the emphasis on Christ's humanity has dimmed our devotion to his divinity.

Matthew 3:7

When he [John the Baptist] saw many of the Pharisees and Sadducees coming to his baptism, he said to them, "You brood of vipers! Who warned you to flee from the coming wrath?"

Meditations & Lessons

✦ In the Old Testament, the Jews would suffer the "wrath" of God again and again after a period of unfaithfulness. But God is merciful rather than vengeful. It is likely that ordinary calamities were often interpreted as God's wrath by guilty consciences. In any event, John saw the Pharisees as being guilty in God's sight.

✦ John had faith in the power of God's mercy so that he knew repentance would save the Pharisees. Perhaps John harbored some vengeful thoughts and thought that the Pharisees should be punished. Yet his faith in God's mercy was strong. He accepted whatever God's grace had led the Pharisees to do.

Matthew 3:13-14

Then Jesus came from Galilee to John at the Jordan to be baptized by him. John tried to prevent him, saying, "I need to be baptized by you, and yet you are coming to me?"

MEDITATIONS & LESSONS

✦ There was an essential difference in the baptism of John and Christ, and yet the question does point out that the minister of the sacrament plays an important role. This is more evident in an adult baptism. In infant baptism, the minister should have a profound effect upon the adults who are involved. There should be something spiritually special about the minister of a sacrament, which will make the sacrament all the more attractive and effective for the people.

✦ The minister of the sacrament can learn much, and grow in faith by observing and appreciating the faith of the recipients. "If they have such great faith in what I am doing, should I not have greater faith myself in what I am doing (and not accept it as routine)? Should I not try to develop greater holiness, to be more 'worthy' of what I am doing, to increase the faith of believers, and spark faith in those who tend to receive the sacraments in a routine manner?"

MATTHEW 8:26-27

Then he got up, rebuked the winds and the sea, and there was great calm. The men were amazed and said, "What sort of man is this, whom even the winds and sea obey?"

MEDITATIONS & LESSONS

✦ We have always been instructed that the miracles were performed to prove that Christ is God. That is a major reason why these miracles were recorded in Scripture. Surely this view seems to have validity.

+ Scripture scholars today, however, tell us that Christ was trying to bring the people back from their semi-pagan ways to worship God in spirit and truth. The major purpose of the miracles was to give them a lively faith in God, who alone could make the Universe with all its beauty and likewise intervene at anytime as well.

+ People today are willing to accept Jesus as having much to offer us, but they don't believe in God or believe that God has an effective influence in the world. We are faced with the same question that Christ faced, not proving his divinity so much as moving people to believe in God.

MATTHEW 9:10-11

While he was at table in his house, many tax collectors and sinners came and sat with Jesus and his disciples. The Pharisees saw this and said to his disciples, "Why does your teacher eat with tax collectors and sinners?"

MEDITATIONS &LESSONS

+ The answer to the question is given very clearly in subsequent verses. Christ came to save sinners, not the righteous. We must remember what the questioners had forgotten; we are all sinners.

+ This sometimes embarrassing problem can face priests and bishops. We are asked to give invocations and then wine and dine with politicians, business and industry leaders, the wealthy, or social climbers, who may not be exemplars of the Christian life. The example of Jesus indicates that we should accept such invitations, but we should do our best to make the presence of Christ felt and not appear to be the tools of "sinners."

Matthew 9:14

Then the disciples of John approached him and said, "Why do we and the Pharisees fast [much], but your disciples do not fast?"

Meditations & Lessons

✦   Obviously the sacrificial life is better than a gluttonous life, but neither fasting nor eating are virtuous or sinful in themselves. One is to live virtuously in keeping with his calling. No one is called to gluttony, of course, but very few seem to be given the grace to lead an extremely sacrificial life such as the Carthusians. Moderation is the key, and penance that extends beyond moderation is more virtuous. God does not ask us to do penance for the sake of penance, but for the sake of the Kingdom.

✦   There are different vocations and careers, for which God, through his providence, has suited each one of us. So, it is not to our credit that we happen to have one vocation/career or another. However, it is to our "credit" to live that vocation/career as it was meant to be lived.

✦   It is possible to find much good even among those who lead less than virtuous lives. The Pharisees, for example, fasted and tithed which are morally good acts. Our mission is to appeal to the better instincts of everyone in order to have them turn their hearts to God. Every person created by God has the possibility for such conversion and the greatest sinners may become the greatest saints—Paul and Augustine are good examples. So ours is not to judge. We should recognize and make our appeal to what is good in the person, inviting him to dedicate that goodness to the service of God.

Matthew 11:2-3

When John heard in prison the works of the Messiah, he sent his disciples to him with this question, "Are you the one who is to come, or should we look for another?"

Meditations & Lessons

✦   We face the same question today. If we did not, there would be no need of faith. A few years ago, we used to answer that the miracles proved that Christ was the Messiah. We still do. But as we look at the condition of our world, we understand more and more that the proof that Jesus is Messiah is the one he gives to John. "Go and tell John what you hear and see: the blind regain their sight, the lame walk, lepers are cleansed, the deaf hear, the dead are raised, and the poor have the good news proclaimed to them. And blessed is the one who takes no offense at me."

✦   The greatest miracle of all is having the key to the mystery of life. How are we to live in this world? Left to ourselves, we would be worse off than Job. But Christ gives the paradoxical answer that we overcome the world by giving rather than receiving, by love, by the corporal and spiritual works of mercy.

✦   It is the tendency of human beings always to be looking "for another". The divorce rate, the numbers leaving priesthood and religious life, the number of "pop" heroes and heroines that we have, are indications. We are all looking for a savior, someone to make us happy now, in this world. Even those who know better often do this. We have our Savior. His message is the secret to happiness not only in the next world, but in this one as well. We need faith, patience, and perseverance.

MATTHEW 12:10

[They questioned him,] "Is it lawful to cure on the sabbath?"

MEDITATIONS & LESSONS

✦   Today, people do not question if it is lawful to heal on the sabbath. Instead, they question whether to believe that God will heal us of physical infirmities. Some people believe all too easily, while some refuse to believe at all. Many others are hesitant. They believe it is possible for God to heal, but they think that sometimes healings are the result of extreme emotionalism rather than the power of God. They fear that when the emotionalism passes, the infirmity may return, and their faith will be crushed or turned to cynicism.

✦   We understand from the teaching of Christ that we are permitted to do almost anything on Sunday as long as it is for a good reason. But we fail to realize that there is still every reason to set aside one day each week to worship God and to rest. The Commandments of God and the Church still very much apply.

✦   Psychological rest is as important as physical relaxation, and we understand today that rest can include strenuous labor. When the vast majority earned their living by physical labor, this type of work was normally to be avoided on Sunday. Now that as many or more people earn a living by sitting at a desk, physical labor can be psychologically restful.

✦   It is important to remember that the Lord's Day is to be devoted to people rather than to work. It should be devoted to God himself and to our families and friends—so that our love for them will be renewed in mind and heart. That way, we will be ready to give of ourselves for another week of work.

MATTHEW 12:23

All the crowd was astounded, and said, "Could this perhaps be the Son of David?"

MEDITATIONS & LESSONS

✦   We need to ask this question with regard to individual charismatics. We should not just lump them into a negative category. There may seem to be undue emotionalism among charismatics, but we must ask if one of them is specially chosen by God to give us inspiration and direction. It is easier to discern God's special inspiration in Popes, the late Mother Teresa and others because clearly the authority of the Church is with them. It is more difficult to recognize the authenticity of those who work more on the fringe of the structure of Christ's Church, but God could be gracing them too.

MATTHEW 13:10

"Why do you speak to them in parables?"

MEDITATIONS & LESSONS

✦   Stories have always been a most appropriate way for a teacher to explain a truth. And most of the time the context in which the story is told reveals its meaning. If not, then the story should peak one's curiosity to ask about it. Christ's listeners could have understood the meaning of the parables in either way. Some were so obvious from the context that it was only the hardness of their hearts, their prejudice that kept them from grasping the meaning.

+ Sometimes, we don't understand what is said because we don't want to. And sometimes we don't seek an explanation because we fear that the answer might force a change in our lives.

+ Christ also spoke in parables so that the innocent, unsophisticated, and humble person could understand him.

MATTHEW 13:54-56

He came to his native place and taught the people in their synagogue. They were astonished and said, "Where did this man get such wisdom and mighty deeds? Is he not the carpenter's son? Is not his mother named Mary and his brothers James, Joseph, Simon, and Judas? And are not his sisters all with us? Where did this man get all this?"

MEDITATIONS & LESSONS

+ It is from such verses as this that scholars of past ages have believed that Jesus, as man, possessed infused knowledge and/or experienced the Beatific Vision. It is surely difficult for modern scholars to put this verse aside. In translation, at least the implication seems to be that Jesus is not only more learned than his "brothers and sisters," but also he has such remarkable wisdom and miraculous power that it is all the more incredible, when one considers his background. Jesus' contemporaries would find it most difficult, if the son of a doctor of the law had such powers, but totally incredible for an uneducated carpenter's son.

+ We have a tendency to judge "home products," because we knew them when. It is good to have a certain skepticism of any human being, and Christ was human. It is especially good for the "home product" himself; it reduces pride and increases humility.

✦   It is unfair to judge a person on the basis of his parents' reputation or that of his brothers and sisters. It is equally unfair to base our judgments on the way a person was years ago. In their youth, some people acquire negative nicknames such as "fatty" or "dopey." (Sometimes these nicknames become self-fulfilling prophecies.) These labels are unfair. To other adolescents, a negative nickname may have seemed to fit the person at one time, but it should not follow him for the rest of his life.

MATTHEW 15:1-2

Then Pharisees and scribes came to Jesus from Jerusalem and said, "Why do your disciples break the tradition of the elders? They do not wash [their] hands when they eat a meal."

MEDITATIONS & LESSONS

✦   We should not confuse man-made traditions with God's law. God's law is unchanging, but man-made traditions can be changed, and they must be changed when they interfere with such essential Christian actions as charity. This was one of the basic premises of Vatican Council II. The bark of Peter had become encrusted with the barnacles of man-made tradition (for example, too much clericalism) and if it was to keep afloat and continue to sail in the type of sea in which we find ourselves, it was necessary that the barnacles be removed.

✦   As Jesus tells us, a person's outer appearance should not prevent us from discovering what the person may be truly like. Outward appearance is in many instances a sign of a person's inner dispositions, but not always. Appearances can be quickly and easily changed. If we look beyond the surface of a poor outward appearance, we may discover a person with a wonderful interior life. The reverse, of course, can be true also.

The person with the good outer appearance can be the source of much evil. Good or evil comes from inside a person.

MATTHEW 15:7-9, 12

"Hypocrites, well did Isaiah prophesy about you when he said:
   'This people honors me with their lips,
   but their hearts are far from me;
   in vain do they worship me,
   teaching as doctrines human precepts.' "
Then his disciples approached and said to him, "Do you know that the Pharisees took offense when they heard what you said?"

MEDITATIONS & LESSONS:

✦ Sometimes the truth hurts.

✦ The correction of another person always "hurts" that person a little bit, but ultimately truth is more important than hurt feelings. If a person is in error, it is charitable to correct the person and uncharitable to leave the person in his error.

✦ Anyone who is offended by the truth, rather than elated by it, is in serious spiritual difficulty. It takes humility to accept the truth. Christ gave the Pharisees something to think about, and allowed them to perceive the truth for themselves. In their stubbornness and pride, they would not even give consideration to his words because he had "hurt" them.

MATTHEW 15:32-33

"My heart is moved with pity for the crowd, for they have been with me now for three days and have nothing to eat. I do not

want to send them away hungry, for fear they may collapse on the way." The disciples said to him, "Where could we ever get enough bread in this deserted place to satisfy such a crowd?"

MEDITATIONS & LESSONS

✦   These few verses seem to show that the Disciples were better disposed toward the crowds than other references would seem to indicate. They were prepared to serve, but had nothing to offer. They seem to identify with Christ's compassion. Still, they do not recognize Christ as God and there is no comment to that effect after the miracle. The point of the story, therefore, seems to be to stress Christ's love for every person, friend or stranger, and the need for the Disciples to think in the same way.

MATTHEW 17:10

"Why do the scribes say that Elijah must come first?"

MEDITATIONS & LESSONS

✦   The Disciples took Scripture seriously and very literally. It is appropriate that we should do the same. Certainly there will be many times when we realize that the Scripture passage is metaphorical, but in order to appreciate the metaphor, we must know something about the literal meaning of words as well. Without the literal meaning, we would not be able to reach the figurative meaning. Both are required.

✦   God always gives us more than enough time to get ready for hardships. We can never say that we were not warned. That is clear in Scripture. It is clear in my personal life, as well. But the warning so often seems hidden from our eyes and is identifiable only on hindsight. Why? Because we have been so preoccupied with ourselves and our own interests, we have not been paying that much attention to what God is telling us.

Matthew 17:19

"Why could we not drive it out?"

Meditations & Lessons

✦ In the time of Jesus, evils that afflicted a person (illness, injury) were attributed to an evil spirit. So not all the cures in the Gospels are miracles in a proper sense (although the suddenness of most of them would be miraculous). Many of their ills could have been overcome by the people themselves, if they were inspired by faith in God, rather than dejected by their belief in the power of evil spirits.

✦ Even today, the chances of recovering good health are hindered when a person despairs because he believes that he is in the grip of an evil spirit. There is a much better chance of recovery for the person who accepts the ailment as a part of Providence and believes that God in his goodness will restore him to health.

✦ Jesus told the Disciples that they were unable to drive the demon from the youth "because of your little faith". Faith is essential. When the doctors fail, when expensive machines fail, when medicines fail, when their self-centered "prayers" fail, people ask the same question. "Why?" Maybe it is best in God's plan that we have the ailment. And if we are to recover, our act of faith should include a purpose of amending our lives and using our restored health to serve God better. What we most often lack is a decision to amend our lives.

MATTHEW 17:24

When they came to Capernaum, the collectors of the temple tax approached Peter and said, "Doesn't your teacher pay the temple tax?"

MEDITATIONS & LESSONS

+ Like Jesus, we who are baptized should live free of obligations to secular power. However, because we are also members of the secular society, we should be good citizens in every way, paying our taxes, and fulfilling our other obligations. But we should remember that we are not of this world. The secular power should have no control over our allegiance to God and the way that we worship him. Our perspective is not that we are primarily citizens of this world, who receive permission from the State to worship. On the contrary, we are children of God who, for reasons of good order, agree to fulfill obligations to the State.

+ Today in the United States, we are urged to have particular qualities (for example, honesty), and we are also urged not to give the impression of the opposite. Jesus acted in the same way two thousand years ago. He had no obligation to pay the tax—or to be circumcised or baptized—but rather than seem like a law breaker, he followed the civil and religious proscriptions of the time.

MATTHEW 18:1

At that time the disciples approached Jesus and said, "Who is the greatest in the kingdom of heaven?"

MEDITATIONS & LESSONS

✦ The greatest in the Kingdom of Heaven is God. No other rank means anything. Everyone in the Kingdom of Heaven is great because they are without sin, totally detached from the world, single-mindedly worshiping God.

✦ Even though human beings will remain sinful right up to the end, we must have a certain "innocence" of children. That is, we must honestly admit to our fault no matter how serious, ask for forgiveness, and then express great love toward the Person who has forgiven us.

✦ The worst type of sin is to lead someone else into sin. The explanation is not given but surely two factors are important: a) once I have led a person into sin, I have no power to get him out again; it depends on his free will. I can try to assist him, but my protestations will lack credibility, b) I have been directly working against God in the service of evil. Even in my most deliberate sin, I have some "human" excuse, because I am working for my pleasure whose appetite can deceive me. In deliberately leading another to sin, the only satisfaction or pleasure is to revel in the evil itself.

MATTHEW 18:21

"Lord, if my brother sins against me, how often must I forgive him? As many as seven times?"

MEDITATIONS & LESSONS

✦ Christ's answer is very difficult to accept because it seems that some people will never reform their ways and that they will keep committing the same sin over and over again. This may be true, but when Jesus speaks about the man whose debt was forgiven, but failed to show mercy to another, he indicates that everyone is sinful and in need of mercy. Perhaps the sins of criminals are no more numerous or severe than the secret sins of others. Perhaps the sins of commission of people who commit the same sin again and again are no more numerous or severe than the sins of omission of others. In any event, everyone certainly receives mercy from God time and again, so we should be patient with others as God has been with us.

✦   Actually, the sin is not so much against "me" as it is against God. When a person hurts me in some way, it is more an opportunity for grace than injury. If I wish to accept some act as an offense, that is exactly what it will be and all that it will be. But, if I accept the act in imitation of Christ, it is greatly to my spiritual benefit and to that of the whole Mystical Body.

Matthew 19:3

"Is it lawful for a man to divorce his wife for any cause whatever?"

Meditations & Lessons

✦   Jesus' answer is unequivocal. We should be able to learn from history that this question and many others are as old as man (Jesus points that out). However, we somehow get the idea that we have come upon something new and the new circumstances of our time allow or demand divorce and remarriage. Christ makes it clear that this is not true. The indissolubility of marriage is divine law.

MATTHEW 19:7

They (Pharisees) said to him, "Then why did Moses command that the man give the woman a bill of divorce and dismiss [her]?"

MEDITATIONS & LESSONS

✦   This is a difficult question because Moses was God's prophet. But the answer states that was not God's intention. This was either an exception to God's law or a man-made law.

✦   The answer also includes the words, "unless the marriage is unlawful". Christ was stating not only that whoever divorces and remarries is guilty of adultery, but he is also saying that marriages which are not legal are invalid. These would include bigamous marriages and marriages between relatives.

MATTHEW 19:16

"Teacher, what good must I do to gain eternal life?"

MEDITATIONS & LESSONS

✦   The Ten Commandments are at the heart of a virtuous life. Other things may be required also, but they are the most basic. It is not as if the Commandments were a "check list" of what not to do. It is not as if one could keep the Commandments and earn an automatic guarantee of salvation. The Commandments are a way of life. Love God with one's whole heart and soul; love one's neighbor as oneself. It is this positive aspect that the rich young man had not understood.

✦   The Commandments are sufficient for eternal life, but they remain the minimum all the same. If one studied only enough to get passing grades, he would never get a perfect mark and might, on occasion, fail a subject. The same is true with the Commandments. Taken negatively, they are a minimum standard; they have a very positive side as well, they are a call to perfection.

MATTHEW 19:24-25

"Again I say to you, it is easier for a camel to pass through the eye of a needle than for one who is rich to enter the kingdom of God." When the disciples heard this, they were greatly astonished and said, "Who then can be saved?"

MEDITATIONS & LESSONS

✦   The Jews understood wealth as a blessing from God, a sign of their goodness. Jesus made clear that it can very well be and most often is just the opposite.

✦   Salvation is a gift from God, not a reward that we earn by our own merit. We are urged to pray for the gift of final perseverance. Right up to the very last moment, the verdict is in doubt, if we fail to accept God's grace. God gives his grace to everyone; only those will be saved who have the disposition to receive and use it.

✦   Jesus says, "For human beings, this is impossible, but for God all things are possible." In other words, we can't save ourselves, but God can save us.

MATTHEW 19:27

Then Peter said in reply, "We have given up everything and followed you. What will there be for us?"

MEDITATIONS & LESSONS

✦   If the question was asked in the context of the previous answer, the question undoubtedly bothered Jesus. But if it did, he displayed no impatience. The Disciples should have known that no one can earn salvation or honors from God. After we have done all that we should do, we should recognize that we are still unprofitable servants. The master does not necessarily give a slave a reward for doing his work. If God did not love us, we would be far less than slaves in our relationship to him.

✦   It is difficult to eliminate egotism and come to know the truth about ourselves. That the Apostles gave up everything and followed Jesus was a privilege, a great gift from God, much more than a sacrifice on their part. If only we could see this more clearly now!

✦   Following Jesus is not a favor we do for God but a great favor that he does for us. It is the offer of the best possible opportunity to save our souls. It is a life that brings peace, joy, consolation, and satisfaction, if only we accept this life in the proper spirit. But too often, like the Apostles, we are looking for rewards, even in this life.

MATTHEW 21:9-10

The crowds preceding him and those following kept crying out and saying:
        "Hosanna to the Son of David;
        blessed is he who comes in the name of the Lord;

hosanna in the highest."
And when he entered Jerusalem, the whole city was shaken and asked, "Who is this?"

Meditations & Lessons

✦ The crowd identifies Jesus as a man and as a prophet—a person who gives witness to God—and a holy person. The "Hosannas" would seem to characterize his holiness as superlative.

✦ Today, some theologians will go no further than to stress the humanity of Jesus. So the question *Who is he?* remains important. If we respond in faith that Christ is God, we bind ourselves very strongly to the imperatives of the Gospel.

✦ If we say that Jesus is anything less than God—no matter how great—we let ourselves off the hook. We can pick and choose from the Gospel. We can determine our own religious practice. Although we accept the general principles of Christianity, we are able to distinguish practical cases according to our human insights.

Matthew 21:15-16

When the chief priests and the scribes saw the wondrous things he was doing, and the children crying out in the temple area, "Hosanna to the Son of David," they were indignant and said to him, "Do you hear what they are saying?"

Meditations & Lessons

✦ Although the worldly-wise may show scorn, ordinary people, good and innocent people have an uncanny insight for truth and goodness. It might not avail them much in this world, but their insight does bring a certain security to them and peace of mind.

✦   Today, some theologians try to tell us that Christ was not God and never claimed to be. If that is so, why would the priests and scribes get so excited about the "Hosannas" of little children? It apparently meant something to them, and when it was called to his attention, Jesus did not deny the meaning of their praise and he encouraged it to continue.

MATTHEW 21:20

"(Disciples) How was it that the fig tree withered immediately?"

MEDITATIONS / LESSON

✦   Human beings are more impressed with strange phenomena in nature than they are with those events that we consider "natural." The wonder is how the fig tree grows at all and produces fruit. Almost anything could cause the fig tree to wither. In this case, it withered because of divine power.

✦   It is amazing that Christ must prove his dominion over nature by causing something to die rather than to live. Ultimate dominion consists in bringing something back to life and Jesus did that, too. Human beings are hard to understand at times.

MATTHEW 21:23

The chief priests and the elders of the people approached him as he was teaching and said, "By what authority are you doing these things? And who gave you this authority?"

MEDITATIONS & LESSONS

✦   The question takes for granted that Jesus was saying and doing some unusual things, things that did not seem to be "earthly," things that would require supernatural power, supernatural "authority."

✦   The question also presumes that Christ himself is not that power, even though on several occasions he claimed it. (Many times, too, he invoked the Father, for example, "The Father and I are one.") Clearly their prejudice (hardness of heart) made it next to impossible for them to believe that Jesus was the Messiah.

✦   Jesus tacitly points to a divine authority in his answer, but he wants that answer to come from the priests. A direct answer from him would only spark angry denunciation. But if the priests could be prompted to think, if Jesus could break through their hardness of heart, they might begin to believe. But they were schemers, not thinkers. They only thought of themselves, rather than the implications of the miracles Jesus had performed and the question he was asking. And so, they continued in their unbelief.

MATTHEW 22:15-17

The Pharisees went off and plotted how they might entrap him in speech. They sent their disciples to him, with the Herodians, saying, "Teacher, we know that you are a truthful man and that you teach the way of God in accordance with the truth. And you are not concerned with anyone's opinion, for you do not regard a person's status. Tell us, then, what is your opinion: Is it lawful to pay the census tax to Caesar or not?"

MEDITATIONS & LESSONS

✦   Christ teaches that man belongs to two separate societies on earth, the Church and the State. He indicates that each has rights. From the whole context of Scripture, it is clear that the "rights" of God (Church) are superior to those of men (State), but there should be cooperation between the two, even though they are quite distinct. "Repay to Caesar what belongs to Caesar and to God what belongs to God." (Mt. 22:21)

✦   If people are to live in communities on earth, there must be organization and leadership (authority). Some maintain that this is not true of the Church, which is a community on earth, but their ideas lead to religious chaos. It costs money to provide the organization and services that society demands, so each person should be expected to pay his share of the cost.

MATTHEW 22:23-28

On that day the Sadducees approached him, saying that there is no resurrection. They put this question to him, saying, "Teacher, Moses said, 'If a man dies without children, his brother shall marry his wife and raise up descendants for his brother.' Now there were seven brothers among us. The first married and died and, having no descendants, left his wife to his brother. The same happened with the second and the third, through all seven. Finally the woman died. Now at the resurrection, of the seven, whose wife will she be?"

MEDITATIONS & LESSONS

✦   Our life in heaven will be perfectly centered in God. Although it seems that there would be some relationship between human beings, there will be no dependence. All of our sustenance is to be found in him. Whatever relationship we may have (or not have) with other human beings in heaven, all will be in, through, with, by God. He will be all in all.

✦   Heaven is not a state of natural happiness, which merely continues our earthly existence in a better form—as if we were to lead almost the same kind of life among the dead (The Lord is not God of the dead but of the living).

✦   In heaven, our happiness will depend upon God and not upon others. Our lives on earth are like that, too. Although we may affect others and be affected by them, the important thing, our salvation, will depend upon our relationship with God. We stand alone before God to answer for our own actions. We will be judged on how we fulfilled the responsibility given to us by God in this life.

✦   Sometimes we can be like the Sadducees and be more concerned with winning arguments than discovering the truth. It takes humility to accept correction.

MATTHEW 22:34-36

When the Pharisees heard that he had silenced the Sadducees, they gathered together, and one of them [a scholar of the law] tested him by asking, "Teacher, which commandment in the law is the greatest?"

MEDITATIONS & LESSONS

✦   The Commandments and all of religion can be reduced to one word LOVE. "Love and do what you please," said St. Augustine. The saying is correct, but greatly misunderstood. "If you love me, keep my commandments." Love is not just a statement or wishful thinking. Love makes all-consuming demands on a person. Love calls for sacrifice, self-denial, humility—really all the virtues. Love amounts to the complete acceptance of God's will in all things.

MATTHEW 24:3

As he was sitting on the Mount of Olives, the disciples approached him privately and said, "Tell us, when will this happen, and what sign will there be of your coming, and of the end of the age?"

MEDITATIONS & LESSONS

✦ Many are predicting that the end is imminent. But it is next to impossible to separate the response of Christ in such a way that we have clear answers to the three questions (When will it happen? What sign will there be of your coming? And of the end of the age?). The only safe answer, is to rely on what Jesus says in verse 42: "So too, you also must be prepared, for at an hour you do not expect, the Son of Man will come."

MATTHEW 26:6-8

Now when Jesus was in Bethany in the house of Simon the leper, a woman came up to him with an alabaster jar of costly perfumed oil, and poured it on his head while he was reclining at table. When the disciples saw this, they were indignant and said, "Why this waste?"

Meditations & Lessons

✦ God has given us charge over the goods of this world with the right to use them for our own benefit. But God also wants us to recognize him as Creator. Therefore it is only right that the goods of this world should be used to honor him.

✦ It may be overdoing it to use the goods of the earth to make places of worship luxurious. But certainly it is not overdoing it—nor can it be called wasteful—to use some of this world's goods to give praise and adoration to God. It was right for Jesus to be anointed because he is God; and, therefore, there was no waste.

Matthew 26:14-15

Then one of the Twelve, who was called Judas Iscariot, went to the chief priests and said, "What are you willing to give me if I hand him over to you?"

Meditations & Lessons

✦ Sin is egocentric. It begins with a mentality of, "What's in it for me?" If that is the criterion by which we measure the desirability of an action, we can hardly avoid committing sin frequently. We will rarely be led to an act of virtue by asking, "What's in it for me?" The proper criterion is, "What would God have me to do?"

✦ Sometimes, when tempted to sin, we think that we have a kind of control over God, that, perhaps, he has to forgive us. We think that we can get away with our sinful action, that we can deceive God. Or possibly we think that God will simply overlook whatever we do. Our free will can be a dangerous faculty. It can give us the sense that we are (or should be) totally free of other persons, including God, that neither God nor anyone else has power over us.

MATTHEW 26:17

The disciples approached Jesus and said, "Where do you want us to prepare for you to eat the Passover?"

MEDITATIONS & LESSONS

✦   Clearly, Jesus had no home other than where he was, no family other than the Apostles. The place to eat the Passover was at home with family. Jesus had given up his family for the larger family of mankind in order to fulfill his Father's mission.

✦   The filial relationship between Christ and his Apostles was now excellent. They were ready to do anything for him. They were actually not as strong as they thought they were, but they were willing. Relations between a bishop and priests should be similar. They will be, if the bishop gives himself unstintingly for his people.

MATTHEW 26:21-25

And while they were eating, he said, "Amen, I say to you, one of you will betray me." Deeply distressed at this, they began to say to him one after another, "Surely, it is not I, Lord?" He said in reply, "He who has dipped his hand into the dish with me is the one who will betray me. The Son of Man indeed goes, as it is written of him, but woe to that man by whom the Son of Man is betrayed. It would be better for that man if he had never been born." Then Judas, his betrayer, said in reply, "Surely it is not I, Rabbi?"

MEDITATIONS & LESSONS

✦   Perhaps eleven of the Disciples said, "Surely it is not I" in order to draw praise, or at least a confirmation of their faithfulness, from the Lord. For Judas, the purpose of the question seems to be for self-protection. He hoped that Jesus would be too merciful to condemn him publicly. If that was his strategy, it worked.

✦   If this were truly a question in the minds of the Eleven—it is a good sign. It is an admission that we are all sinners, all capable of treachery towards God. It is good also that they should have asked about themselves (if not selfishly, as above) rather than speculate, trying to point the finger at someone else.

MATTHEW 26:59-62

The chief priests and the entire Sanhedrin kept trying to obtain false testimony against Jesus in order to put him to death, but they found none, though many false witnesses came forward. Finally two came forward who stated, "This man said, 'I can destroy the temple of God and within three days rebuild it.'" The high priest rose and addressed him, "Have you no answer?"

MEDITATIONS & LESSONS

✦   The very silence of Christ was a testimony to his divinity. What right has any person to call him to task, to demand an account from him?

✦   Not every question from every person is worthy of an answer. In this case, the high priest was looking for an argument (which he would gratuitously deny). Christ had already given the best possible answer—

the only answer—his teaching and deeds. If these most remarkable words and deeds had no value as evidence of who he was, argument certainly would not suffice at this point.

MATTHEW 26:62

"What are these men testifying against you?"

MEDITATIONS & LESSONS

✦   Christ allows the prophecy of his Resurrection to stand as the testimony that convicts him as a blasphemer, making the Resurrection all the more valuable as evidence, when it would take place. He could not very well reply to this question except to say, "Wait and see." In light of events, that was what his silence said. He could give no further or greater signs of divinity than he had already given except for the Resurrection, "the sign of Jonah!"

MATTHEW 26:63-65

Then the high priest said to him, "I order you to tell us under oath before the living God whether you are the Messiah, the Son of God." Jesus said to him in reply, "You have said so. But I tell you:

> *From now on you will see the 'Son of Man*
> *seated at the right hand of the Power'*
> *and 'coming on the clouds of heaven.' "*

Then the high priest tore his robes and said. "He has blasphemed! What further need have we of witnesses?"

MEDITATIONS & LESSONS

✦ It is clear from their customs that, in the trial of Jesus, they were operating outside their own law in different ways. They wanted the witnesses as a cover; long ago they had made their determination that Jesus was guilty. So often human beings arrive at a decision first and look for information or proof later. That is not the way to discover truth, but to reinforce prejudice.

MATTHEW. 26:65-66

"You have heard the blasphemy; what is your opinion?"

MEDITATIONS & LESSONS

✦ It is well to act with caution when it becomes necessary to make judgments about individuals and their words and deeds. Caution is necessary even though it may prolong a situation—sometimes even causing harm to a community—and give the impression that the offending person may be "getting away with murder". While trying to limit harm to the community, we should be gracious and merciful in our judgements concerning the offending individual, just as God is. It is not our judgment that counts in the final analysis, but God's judgement. Rushing to judgment can produce a great injustice.

MATTHEW 26:67-68

Then they spat in his face and struck him, while some slapped him, saying, "Prophesy for us, Messiah: who is it that struck you?"

MEDITATIONS & LESSONS

✦ When mob psychology takes over, a nasty vindictiveness is released. In the long run, it is not the innocent victim who is hurt most in such a situation but the members of the mob. The individual in the mob is either further convinced of his prejudiced action and therefore continues in error, or he later realizes his guilt and is tormented by it. The major suffering of the innocent is disappointment in the blindness of some people.

✦ Our sins make all of us part of the crowd. We think that our sins are hidden, and perhaps they are hidden from the world, but the Lord knows who we are. But even if he did not, our sins do not have the detrimental effect on him that they have on us.

MATTHEW 27:3-4

Then Judas, his betrayer, seeing that Jesus had been condemned, deeply regretted what he had done. He returned the thirty pieces of silver to the chief priests and elders, saying, "I have sinned in betraying innocent blood." They said, "What is that to us?"

MEDITATIONS & LESSONS

✦ A rhetorical question was the response to the lament of Judas that he had betrayed innocent blood. The chief priests and the elders accepted no responsibility for the evil done. It mattered not whether Christ were innocent. They had arranged a business deal with Judas and, having kept their part of the bargain, they were free of guilt.

✦ So often we can have the same response to the betrayal of innocent life, whether near home, or especially in more distant places. Why should we say anything about it? What can we do anyway? Better to mind our own business. We fail to realize that if one member of the body politic suffers, all of us suffer with him. Society has been further impoverished by the act. To minimize the harm, or perhaps to bring great good out of the evil, we do have an obligation to say and to do what we can.

MATTHEW 27:11

Now Jesus stood before the governor, and he questioned him, "Are you the king of the Jews?"

MEDITATIONS & LESSONS

   ✦   Christ had not used that title himself, although he had spoken of his Kingdom. Now he clearly accepts the title bestowed upon him. His Kingdom, of course, is much broader. He may well have given the same response, if Pilate had asked him whether or not he was king of the Romans.

   ✦   If this terminology had not been used, chances are that Pilate would not have examined the case as carefully as he did.

MATTHEW 27:12-13

When he was accused by the chief priests and elders, he made no answer. Then Pilate said to him, "Do you not hear how many things they are testifying against you?"

MEDITATIONS & LESSONS

   ✦   Often, not only in courts but in other matters, the quantity rather than the quality of testimony can have an overwhelming influence on the outcome of a case. Christ was not about to dignify testimony that was obviously false with an answer.

✦   Not only the Jews but Pilate himself knew what had been going on in Jerusalem and other areas of Palestine. It was Pilate's business to know. Justice would require that Pilate rule as inadmissible any evidence that was contrary to his reports, or suspend judgment until he could check the charges.

MATTHEW 27:15-17

Now on the occasion of the feast the governor was accustomed to release to the crowd one prisoner whom they wished. And at that time they had a notorious prisoner called [Jesus] Barabbas. So when they had assembled, Pilate said to them, "Which one do you want me to release to you, [Jesus] Barabbas, or Jesus called Messiah?"

MEDITATIONS & LESSONS

✦   Truth and justice are rarely arrived at through majority vote. It is patient research, analysis of facts and testimony that are needed. Emotion can and does block reason.

✦   It is not that the judge is any smarter than the others, but he has the responsibility. The judge must not abdicate that responsibility because there is never any assurance, in fact, quite the contrary, that others will act responsibly.

✦   Pilate had the dangerously proud idea that his office gave a supreme power, not merely to judge, but to dispose of human life as he saw fit, even if he acted in an arbitrary manner. Apparently, those in power saw themselves as having certain powers that only God possesses.

Matthew 27:19-21

While he was still seated on the bench, his wife sent him a message, "Have nothing to do with that righteous man. I suffered much in a dream today because of him. The chief priests and the elders persuaded the crowds to ask for Barabbas but to destroy Jesus. The governor said to them in reply, "Which of the two do you want me to release to you?"

Meditations & Lessons

✦   There are times, when we are about to commit a serious wrong, that we get a chance to change our mind. This was the case for Pilate and also for the crowd. And yet, because of free will, we can ignore the opportunity to avoid evil and reconfirm our action.

Matthew 27:22

Pilot said to them, "Then what shall I do with Jesus called Messiah?"

Meditations & Lessons

✦   Pilate has turned the power to judge over to the crowd. In effect, he is consenting to mob rule.

✦   Obviously, the reaction of the crowd convinced Pilate, to act against his better judgment (and his wife's). There is every indication that God gave Pilate the opportunity and the grace to reach the conclusion that he was wrongly condemning Jesus to death.

Matthew 27:22-23

They all said, "Let him be crucified." But he said, "Why? What evil has he done?"

Meditations & Lessons

✦ Apparently Pilate saw no evil in Jesus and realized that his condemnation was unjust. He was perfectly agreeable to having Jesus killed, but he wanted a reason, some kind of rationale for the condemnation.

✦ We sometimes make a decision before having all the facts. Out of fear or pride or the desire to please others, we act unfairly, listening to only one side of the story and being deaf and blind to any contrary evidence that is brought forward. This can happen not only in police investigations, but in our personal lives as well.

Chapter Six

Questions Others asked in the Gospel of Mark

Mark 1:23-24

In their synagogue was a man with an unclean spirit; he cried out, "What have you to do with us, Jesus of Nazareth? Have you come to destroy us?"

Meditations & Lessons

✦   That was exactly Jesus' mission in the world, to destroy the grip that evil had upon human beings. It was not to be an absolute destruction—there was still to be a test for man—but Christ destroyed evil for those who wish to be free of it.

✦   Those who wish to dabble with evil, may do so, but they have only themselves to blame for what happens.

MARK 1:26-27

The unclean spirit convulsed him and with a loud cry came out of him. All were amazed and asked one another, "What is this? A new teaching with authority. He commands even the unclean spirits and they obey him."

MEDITATIONS & LESSONS

✦   The teaching was not so new as the Teacher. Here was One teaching with authority! The question was rhetorical, one of reverential awe. It was obvious that the teaching they heard had a new force and urgency because of who the teacher was.

✦   According to Mark's gospel, it seems clear that Jesus was "instantaneously" recognizable as the Messiah. Right from the beginning of his ministry, the people could detect something extraordinary about the Man, even if they had only been in his presence once.

✦   Any doubts that people had concerning him were imprudent doubts. His very person, his words, his actions were unmistakable. What they needed was the gift of faith to accept what their senses told them.

MARK 2:5-7

When Jesus saw their faith, he said to the paralytic, "Child, your sins are forgiven." Now some of the scribes were sitting there asking themselves, "Why does this man speak that way? He is blaspheming."

MEDITATIONS & LESSONS

✦   Since the scribes called Christ's words and actions blasphemy, they obviously recognized that Jesus was claiming to be God. And when he consistently made the same claim in diverse ways, they should have tested the claim. When they did test him, they could never find him in error. They should have continued their investigation or admitted that he was the Messiah.

✦   The scribes chose a completely illogical alternative—they decided that he was not the Messiah and not from God, and, therefore, worthy of death, despite all the evidence to the contrary.

MARK 2:7

"Who but God alone can forgive sins?"

MEDITATIONS & LESSONS

✦   Full forgiveness of sins is God's prerogative alone, a sure sign of divinity. But it is easy to say the words. Jesus proved that he had that power by having a cripple arise and walk. Surely this sign must have shaken the scribes and caused them to wonder, and perhaps even to believe. "They were all astounded and glorified God, saying, 'We have never seen anything like this!' "

✦   Surely, if there is a God, and man is gifted with freedom to act virtuously or sinfully, it seems absolutely necessary that a loving God would institute some system for the forgiveness of sins. In other religions, the people plead for mercy and forgiveness. The Catholic Church is the only one that claims to possess the power from God to forgive sins. If it stands to reason that God should grant this power, it stands to reason that the Catholic Church is the one true Church of God.

MARK 2:16

Some scribes who were Pharisees saw that he was eating with sinners and tax collectors and said to his disciples, "Why does he eat with tax collectors and sinners?"

MEDITATIONS & LESSONS

✦   It is not wrong in our day to eat and associate with those whose chief priority is wealth, as long as we speak very directly to them about evil. If we are going to approve their positions tacitly by our silence, that is wrong, but if we are going to try to convert them to moral principle and concern for the poor, that is a great service. Besides, if we have the obvious great concern for the poor that Christ had, there can hardly be any complaint, just look at how people reacted to Mother Teresa.

✦   Judgment as to whether or not a person is a sinner is God's prerogative, not man's. In our associations with others, we do not need to be concerned so much with the other person's possible sinfulness. We need to be concerned with our own virtue and our own manner of conduct in relation to every person.

MARK 2:18

"Why do the disciples of John and the disciples of the Pharisees fast, but your disciples do not fast?"

MEDITATIONS & LESSONS

✦   When asked this question, Jesus tries once again to make the point that he is not an "ordinary prophet." He is the object of all prophecy; he is the goal of all those who fast. So while he is present, fasting would be a contradiction. The purpose of fasting is to purify oneself of temporal concerns so that one may be more perfectly united to God. When he is already present, fasting becomes unnecessary.

✦ Positive acts of virtue are even more important than penance, although the two ordinarily are complimentary. In order to have the opportunity to pray, we may need to mortify ourselves in some way. But prayer is more important than mortification. If an act of penance leads to uncharitable conduct (like making one testy) rather than to virtue, it is a sign that the penance is performed as a matter of personal pride, rather than in an effort to move closer to God.

MARK 2:23-24

As he was passing through a field of grain on the sabbath, his disciples began to make a path while picking the heads of grain. At this the Pharisees said to him, "Look, why are they doing what is unlawful on the sabbath?"

MEDITATIONS & LESSONS

✦ The Lord alone can declare what is or is not lawful on the sabbath. He commands that we keep holy the sabbath day, but the practical ordinances have been developed by human beings.

✦ The Pharisees were more interested in protecting their own authority than having the sabbath kept holy. Indeed, various exceptions are permitted when some necessity arises.

Mark 4:37-38

A violent squall came up and waves were breaking over the boat, so that it was already filling up. Jesus was in the stern, asleep on a cushion. They woke him and said to him, "Teacher, do you not care that we are perishing?"

Meditations & Lessons

✦   Jesus cared very much for his Apostles; examples abound. But, as God, he had no fear of anything in the world. He cared not about the strength of the elements; he did care for the Apostles. On the other hand, he would not be bothered by their perishing because the Lord saw with perfect clarity that this would be the beginning of eternal life, something not to be feared but welcomed.

Mark 4:41

They were filled with great awe and said to one another, "Who then is this whom even wind and sea obey?"

Meditations & Lessons

✦   There was no question that the miracles of Jesus and the manner in which they were accomplished proved beyond doubt that Jesus was of God. If it were possible for the Apostles to think in such terms before the Resurrection, they would have recognized Christ as God himself. Peter's declaration was made before the Resurrection, but the Apostles really did not understand its full truth until later. After the Resurrection, Jesus' many words and deeds, in hindsight, were recognized as proof of his divinity.

✦ We can see from this episode perhaps why God tolerates free will in man. The wind and the sea had no choice but to obey their Creator. There is no worship in their "obedience." To truly give honor and glory to God, we creatures should do so freely; and our obedience as human beings should be prompt and fully compliant. We should be as ready as the wind and the waves—more so because of our intelligence—to obey God's commands. And yet, we fail to do so. This is strange indeed, a creature disobeying the Creator! It is a total distortion of what should be.

MARK 5:35

"While he was still speaking, people from the synagogue official's house arrived and said, "Your daughter has died; why trouble the teacher any longer?"

MEDITATIONS & LESSONS

✦ Let the Teacher (God) decide. No question is ever too foolish. The good teacher accepts every question, because each offers a new way of looking at a subject. The explanation might help not only the questioner but others as well—those who think that they understand but may understand more perfectly with a further explanation. In this case, it is obvious that none of those present understood the power of Christ. They did not understand much more after he miraculously brought the little girl back to life, but it was another demonstration of the power of Jesus.

MARK 6:2

When the sabbath came he began to teach in the synagogue, and many who heard him were astonished. They said, "Where did this man get all this? What kind of wisdom has been given him?"

MEDITATIONS & LESSONS

✦   The people made very little effort to answer their own questions. The questions were the correct ones, but they needed to be pursued. Christ had great power and wisdom, unusual for any person. Where did it come from? And if it was super-human, where did he come from? Who was he?

✦   Often enough, we refuse to listen. Bishops should test what the charismatics have to offer. Maybe there is a message. Vatican II has asked us to test even what atheists have to offer, because they may provide us with valuable insights, or at least with an insight as to how we might approach them. Surely, all of our people should listen more patiently to the Holy See, to the Council, to the Bishops' Conferences, even to the local Bishop, more than they do. It is not a matter of instant inspiration but over the long haul, if we listen and reflect on what we hear, God will speak the truth to us through human instruments.

MARK 6:3

"Is he not the carpenter, the son of Mary, and the brother of James and Joseph and Judas and Simon? And are not his sisters here with us?"

MEDITATIONS & LESSONS

✦   Much as we like to point to the miracles of Christ as proof of his divinity, they do seem to have the same characteristics that are associated with the charismatics. Great faith is needed on the part of the recipient. Could these be "faith healings"? Perhaps some, but not all.

✦ In any event, although some miracles might seem to be a *conditio sine qua non* for divinity, it would seem that Christ's holiness, his wisdom, and the way in which his life and actions fulfilled prophecy maybe even stronger testimony to His divinity.

MARK 6:37

He said to them in reply, "Give them some food yourselves." But they said to him, "Are we to buy two hundred days' wages worth of food and give it to them to eat?"

MEDITATIONS & LESSONS

✦ "What about us?" seems to be the cry of the Apostles. They did not have much money in the common purse; these people had no real claim on them. It was just a coincidence, some hungry people with Christ and the Apostles. Could they do anything for them? Were they willing to do anything for them? Their implied response is negative.

✦ Our own reaction to similar opportunities, whether collections or sharing what we have, is ordinarily the same as the Apostles. We are willing to give something, but why should the whole burden fall on our shoulders? It is not fair. It should not happen this way. Jesus' reply is to do what we can and go as far as possible, anyway.

MARK 7:5

The Pharisees and scribes questioned him, "Why do your disciples not follow the tradition of the elders but instead eat a meal with unclean hands?"

Meditations & Lessons

   ✦   Those who hold to tradition in one area may very well be making more serious errors in another. Witness the traditionalists who oppose the Vatican Council. They are self-righteous. They may have a few well-taken points, but overall, they are defiant on the most important truths of tradition.

   ✦   The Disciples were being taught to accept the most ancient of traditions: a) Believe in the Messiah; and b) Love God wholeheartedly and love your neighbor as yourself. They also observed just about every other tradition—or at least we see Christ doing so—with regard to worship. "Violations" came, when there was some over-riding concern for human life, which did not diminish God's glory but evidenced goodness and love.

   ✦   Note that the Pharisees speak of the "tradition of the elders" and not of Divine Law. Perhaps this phrase included the Law and the prophets in some way, but there was more emphasis on man-made tradition than there was on the Law.

Mark 8:2-4

"My heart is moved with pity for the crowd, because they have been with me now for three days and have nothing to eat. If I send them away hungry to their homes, they will collapse on the way, and some of them have come a great distance." His disciples answered him, "How can anyone get enough bread to satisfy them here in this deserted place?"

Meditations & Lessons

   ✦   The narration is so matter-of-fact that one has the impression that this did happen more than once and Christ allowed the repetition in order to make a greater impression on the Apostles at the Last Supper. Perhaps the miracle of multiplying loaves and fishes was repeated several times in order that the miracle of the Eucharist would mean more and more to them as time went on.

MARK 9:9-11

As they were coming down from the mountain, he charged them not to relate what they had seen to anyone, except when the Son of Man had risen from the dead. So they kept the matter to themselves, questioning what rising from the dead meant. Then they asked him, "Why do the scribes say that Elijah must come first?"

MEDITATIONS & LESSONS

✦   It is not necessarily Elijah but one like him who must come. Often St. John the Baptist is mentioned in this regard. Again, however, the Jews were looking for a great sign, one that they would dictate rather than one determined by God himself. If God met their "demands," as it were, they would accept him; otherwise not.

MARK 9:28

"Why could we not drive it out?"

MEDITATIONS & LESSONS

✦   The Disciples asked Jesus this question after he had driven an evil spirit out of a boy when they had failed to do so. He told them, "This kind can only come out through prayer." We might ask why we do not have more spiritual success, make more progress in our own time. Could not the answer be that there is not enough prayer?

✦ The Disciples, to be sure, understood that it was through their association with Christ that they had received remarkable powers. Yet they apparently succumbed to the temptation of believing that they could do some things by themselves, that is, without prayer. Is this not true in our own day with regard to our preaching, our organizational efforts, and other things we seek to accomplish?

✦ Another reason for the Disciples' failure may have been that they did not encourage the petitioners to have great faith in God. It could be that the Disciples and the petitioners were placing their trust in the power of human beings and not God who was working through them.

MARK 10:2

The Pharisees approached and asked, "Is it lawful for a husband to divorce his wife?"

MEDITATIONS & LESSONS

✦ No matter how one wishes to interpret Moses, it is clear that Christ's answer to this question is a definitive, emphatic, "No."

✦ Christ's answer also seems to go beyond mere legality (is it lawful) to state that monogamy is the very way in which God has made man and woman; from the very nature of the sexes, from the beginning, from the way that God made them, there is no other possibility.

✦ The way the question is asked—"Is it lawful?"—and answered would indicate that it is impossible for man to change monogamy because God has already established it as a firm rule.

MARK 10:17

"Good teacher, what must I do to inherit eternal life?"

MEDITATIONS & LESSONS

✦   The tragedy of this man seems to be that he recognized quite well who Christ was (Good Teacher) and that it was within his power to grant him eternal life. And despite the fact that the man saw this with such clarity, he refused to follow the advice of Jesus, "You are lacking one thing. Go, sell what you have, and give to the poor and you will have treasure in heaven; then come, follow me." Surely, among all the people of the New Testament, we Americans should be able to identify with this. We know clearly that Christ is God; we know what he expects of us; we find it difficult from a human standpoint to do what he expects of us.

✦   The man saw eternal life as a free gift of God and yet he realized that there must be something God would demand as a condition. It was not necessary for the man to do anything great. He was only asked to place his full trust in God and be kind to others by giving what he had to the poor, such as love of God, love of neighbor.

✦   This story might be connected with the previous one about the children, who have no possessions of their own and must depend completely on the goodness of their parents. We are to be like the little children; "to such belongs the Kingdom of God."

MARK 10:23-26

Jesus looked around and said to his disciples, "How hard it is for those who have wealth to enter the kingdom of God!...It is easier for a camel to pass through [the] eye of [a] needle than for one who

is rich to enter the kingdom of God. "They were exceedingly aston-
ished and said among themselves, "Then who can be saved?"

Meditations & Lessons

  ✦   The Jews thought that material prosperity was a sign of God's blessing, and therefore, a confirmation from God that the rich were also holy, deserving. If the rich would have difficulty getting to Heaven, surely no one else could be saved.

  ✦   Salvation comes from God alone. Jesus said, "For human beings it is impossible, but not for God (verse 25)." No man can earn or deserve it.

  ✦   Goodness does not depend upon how much of this world's goods we may receive or accumulate, but on how we use (give away) what we receive. This reminds us of Christ's remarks about ritual purity. It is not what goes into a man that makes him pure or impure; it is what comes out of him, out of his mind and heart.

Mark 11:27-28

As he was walking in the temple area, the chief priests, the scribes, and the elders approached him and said to him, "By what author-
ity are you doing these things? Or who gave you this authority to do them?"

Meditations & Lessons

  ✦   Those who always test others, who always ask for proof, are rarely satisfied, and they rarely accept the fact that their doubts have been answered. Pride prompts them to ask for so much proof in the first place, and pride will always be a serious obstacle for them to believe the proof which is given.

✦ On the evidence of his actions, the people believed that John the Baptist was sent from God. The priests, scribes, and elders did not accept that evidence. Jesus had given even greater proof that he was sent from God, but it was obvious from their questions to Jesus that the priests, scribes and elders had no intention of opening themselves to the possibility of belief.

✦ Miracles are a powerful proof of Jesus' divinity. But his wisdom and holiness are even greater proof. It was asked, "How did he come by this wisdom?" How, indeed?

✦ The power, by which Jesus acted, was obviously supernatural or preternatural. Therefore, it came either from God or Satan. But since everything Jesus did was completely in accord with God's goodness and not evil in any way, his authority was necessarily that of God.

MARK 12:14

"Is it lawful to pay the census taxes to Caesar or not? Should we pay or should we not pay?"

MEDITATIONS & LESSONS

✦ This is another example of Jesus' enemies testing him. Their failure to trick him or deceive him should have led them to reexamine their disbelief.

✦ Priority, even in this world, should be given to spiritual affairs. For the present, we tolerate the temporal, we do what is necessary for the common good, but we should never be deceived into giving priority to the material and temporal order.

✦   While on earth, the common good is important. In justice we must accept our share of responsibility.

✦   Religion should not be reduced to a matter of collection money. A certain amount of money is necessary for operation, but if we judge the success or failure of a parish based on the cash flow, we are making a sad mistake—yet it happens. It is better to let the State have its money, and it is better for us to develop spirituality.

MARK 12:23

"At the resurrection [when they arise] whose wife will she be?"

MEDITATIONS & LESSONS

✦   The Sadducees probably thought they would outfox Jesus when they asked him about a woman who had been married successively to seven brothers. They wanted to know whose wife she would be at the resurrection. Jesus takes the opportunity to explain something of heaven and tell the Sadducees just how misled they are. The Sadducees discovered that those who think they can outfox Jesus are invariably wrong.

✦   This incident is proof that faith in God's revelation is superior to man's theological musings on it. Theology is good and necessary, but it is so easy to miss the mark that, if we are forced to a choice, simple faith is preferable. In any event, theology without the confirmation of the Church can be dangerously misleading.

✦   This world passes. Not only do cultures change, not only do we use up the goods of the world, not only do we ourselves have a short life span, but everything that the world offers will pass away, and the imperfect will be replaced by the perfect. Those things that we thought on earth to be good, true, and valuable, will be shown to be imperfect, when seen in comparison to the goodness, truth, and beauty of the true God.

MARK 12:28

One of the scribes, when he came forward and heard them disputing and saw how well he had answered them, asked him, "Which is the first of all the commandments?"

MEDITATIONS & LESSON

✦ Basically, everything goes back to the existence of God and his creation of man. If we acknowledge God and his creation, everything else falls into place. If we fail to do this, then our thinking, our philosophy of life is bound to be faulty, no matter how smart we may be.

✦ The purpose of the Commandments is to make life easy, not difficult. If we observe them, the problems of life will always be fleeting. If we violate the Commandments, our problems grow and, in the end, will tend to be incapacitating. A nagging conscience is a burden which can affect our attitude and our judgments. In addition, just trying to cover our tracks will cause us difficulties.

MARK 13:4

"Tell us, when will this happen, and what sign will there be when all these things are about to come to an end?"

MEDITATIONS & LESSONS

✦ This question, asked by four of the Apostles, displays a natural curiosity, rather than anxiety. The Lord was able to use the question to teach several lessons to future generations. The question itself has so little to do with the Gospel, however, that the Lord might not have answered it.

✦   The answer to the question is that sin—rejection of God—brings on disaster not only to individual souls at the end of the world but also to the whole community in the course of time. The innocent suffer with the wicked. The idea of many suffering for the sins of one or a few is not only taught in Genesis but in this passage, and in Paul's words, "If one member of the body suffers, all the other members suffer with him."

✦   Jesus lists a number of signs of the end, all of which have taken place through the centuries. One sign, the enmity between parents and children (verse 12), seems to be growing today. Parental enmity is manifested in birth control, abortion, child abuse. Children's enmity toward their parents includes suits brought by children against their parents for damages suffered in childhood, and not caring for the elderly.

MARK 14:4

"Why has there been this waste of perfumed oil?"

MEDITATIONS & LESSONS

✦   Perhaps ninety-nine times out of one hundred, the objection to extravagance is valid. However, in this case, where a woman was anointing Jesus with expensive perfume, there are three factors we cannot ignore. First, the ointment was used for the Lord of Heaven and earth, Second, Jesus was about to undergo his Passion and death, so this was a suitable time to use perfumed oil. Third, as Jesus tells us, "The poor you will have always with you; and whenever you wish you can do good to them, but you will not always have me."

MARK 14:12

"Where do you want us to go and prepare for you to eat the Passover?"

MEDITATIONS & LESSONS

✦　There was no question as to who was in charge. The Apostles went to Christ to ask for instructions about a matter that could easily have been delegated or handled by Judas without delegation. Maybe they were finally beginning to understand the idea of service.

✦　The Apostles were not asking for themselves. Now that they had the Lord with them, they might not be so particular about observing the Passover. That is not very likely, but the whole context indicates that Jesus was even more particular than they about observing proper ritual.

MARK 14:18-19

Jesus said, "Amen, I say to you, one of you will betray me, one who is eating with me." They began to be distressed and to say to him, one by one, "Surely it is not I?"

MEDITATIONS & LESSONS

✦　It is difficult to know in what manner the question was being asked. Was it from a sense of complete innocence? From a sense of guilt that they had all betrayed Christ in one way or another and wanted him to save them, if they should be guilty? As a test, that he really did not know, or was too kind to identify the guilty one? Since they heard no answer, perhaps they went on with the meal believing that no one would actually betray the Lord or that, if anything, it was a matter of group guilt, something that they had already done or might do through ignorance.

Mark 14:60

The high priest rose before the assembly and questioned Jesus, saying, "Have you no answer? What are these men testifying against you?"

Meditations & Lessons

✦   Jesus saw it as useless and undignified to make a response to what the evangelist saw to be blatantly false testimony. To answer false testimony immediately places one in the position of granting it at least some shred of credibility. Silence did not help his cause, but speech would have engaged him in argument that his opponents could win with numbers, volume and emotion. Christ preferred to let their consciences (they knew that false testimony had been given) be his defense.

Mark 14:61

Again the high priest asked him and said to him, "Are you the Messiah, the son of the Blessed One?" Then Jesus answered, "I am; and 'you will see the Son of Man seated at the right hand of the Power and coming with the clouds of heaven.' "

MEDITATIONS & LESSONS

✦   Jesus answered the question and expanded upon it. The tragedy is that the high priest did not continue questioning him and allow Jesus a full opportunity to explain his mission before the supreme religious body of the land. The assembly might have had a chance to be convinced that Jesus was indeed Messiah. Instead, the high priest condemned him out of hand as blasphemous without any kind of hearing. Given the circumstances, it is obvious that they were not receptive to a Messiah, even though his coming was fundamental to their religious beliefs.

MARK 14:63

At that the high priest tore his garments and said, "What further need have we of witnesses?"

MEDITATIONS & LESSONS

✦   The high priest's actions were a theatrical sham. What he was really saying was, "We have no need of witnesses. Pronounce the decision that we made weeks ago without these idiots and without any trial."

✦   Actually, Jesus admitted that there was no reason for summoning witnesses. Everyone knew what he had been about. Everything was done in the open. The entire city and nation were the courtroom. But what he asked was that they study the evidence and seek the truth.

MARK 15:2

Pilate questioned him, "Are you the king of the Jews?"

Meditations & Lessons

✦　Jesus is King, not only of the Jews, but of all humanity. He is God, Creator of all, and his Kingdom is for everyone. He has not only created man, but has redeemed man and merited man's sanctification.

Mark 15:3-4

The chief priests accused him of many things. Again Pilate questioned him, "Have you no answer?"

Meditations & Lessons

✦　To reply to false accusations is to give them legitimacy, some degree of validity; so Christ remained silent.

Mark 15:8-9

The crowd came forward and began to ask him to do for them as he was accustomed. Pilate answered, "Do you want me to release to you the king of the Jews?"

Meditations & Lessons

✦　Obviously, Pilate was making a grim joke. But the words reveal also that Pilate knew a great deal about Jesus and the reaction of the Jewish leaders to him. It is possible that he asked such a sarcastic question only on the basis of what he had heard and seen that day. But it is much more likely that the question was based on a thorough knowledge of the situation.

✦ Politically this was a key question, and a mistake on Pilate's part, if he were to have any chance of releasing Jesus. Facetious though the question was, it put the Pharisees on the line as being unalterably opposed to the release of Jesus. When "the red banner" was raised, they could do nothing else, but charge at it.

✦ Jesus was condemned by the Sanhedrin for blasphemy. Pilate condemned him for usurping the crown—so the choice was not only between Jesus and Barabbas, but also between Jesus and Herod.

Mark 15:12

Pilate again said to them in reply, "Then what [do you want] me to do with [the man you call] the king of the Jews?"

Meditations & Lessons

✦ By using the title "king of the Jews," Pilot is uttering a terrible irony. He is also pointing to the fact that the great issue is the opposition to the Messiah. The crowd's response, "Crucify him," points to their total rejection of him.

Mark 15:14

Pilate said to them, "Why? What evil has he done?"

Meditations & Lessons

✦ Regardless of what accusations the Jews made, the absence of a response to Pilate's question, shows that neither the Jews nor the more objective Pilate could find that Christ had done anything evil. They were clearly condemning an innocent Person.

MARK 16:2-3

Very early, when the sun had risen, on the first day of the week, they came to the tomb. They were saying to one another, "Who will roll back the stone for us from the entrance to the tomb?"

MEDITATIONS & LESSONS

✦   The holy women's faith in the power of God apparently was not what it could have been—especially since they had witnessed the resurrection of Lazarus and heard Christ's prophecies about himself. Or again, perhaps the prophecies did not register forcefully when they were made, but gained meaning afterwards, and increasingly so until they were written into the Gospels.

CHAPTER SEVEN

Questions Others Asked in the Gospel of Luke

LUKE 1:13-18

But the angel said to him, "Do not be afraid, Zechariah, because your prayer has been heard. Your wife Elizabeth will bear you a son, and you shall name him John"...Then Zechariah said to the angel, "How shall I know this?"

MEDITATIONS & LESSONS

✦   If he was paying attention to the angel, Zechariah should have known that had he had already received a sufficient sign, which is why he was struck speechless. Later on, the Jews also asked for excessive signs, and the Lord refused them, too. Today, we seem to be doing the same thing. We have the Old Testament, Christ, the martyrs, the great saints, the Councils of the Church, etc., and still we fail to believe firmly as we should and act upon our belief. It seems that some calamity must trigger our faith and our actions.

✦   The Lord asks us for faith. He does not ask that we understand everything. If we could understand everything, then we would be as gods.

LUKE 1:30-34

Then the angel said to her, "Do not be afraid, Mary, for you have found favor with God. Behold, you will conceive in your womb and bear a son, and you shall name him Jesus."...But Mary said to the angel, "How can this be, since I have no relations with a man?"

MEDITATIONS & LESSONS

✦   The difference between Mary's question and Zechariah's is that Zechariah asked for a sign at the very moment that he was receiving one. So he was given one that he did not like. Mary was asking for a further explanation. Her question can even be understood as asking for instructions, such as, 'How do you want me to go about this, what must I do, since I have no husband?'

LUKE 1:41-43

When Elizabeth heard Mary's greeting, the infant leaped in her womb, and Elizabeth, filled with the holy Spirit, cried out in a loud voice and said, "Most blessed are you among women and blessed is the fruit of your womb. And how does this happen to me, that the mother of my Lord should come to me?"

Meditations & Lessons

✦ All guests should be received in the same way that Elizabeth welcomed Mary. Guests are sisters and brothers of Christ.

✦ If Elizabeth should be so excited about Mary's visit, what should be our state of mind and wonder that Christ should come to us in the Eucharist and be available for visits every minute of the day?

✦ We should not dwell too long on the "why" or the "how." Instead, we should simply take advantage of the privilege that is ours through faith. Faith is far greater, far more valuable than reason in this regard.

Luke 1:65-66

Then fear came upon all their neighbors, and all these matters were discussed throughout the hill country of Judea. All who heard these things took them to heart, saying, "What, then, will this child be?"

Meditations & Lessons

✦ Elizabeth was beyond child-bearing age. The baby's parents were breaking tradition by naming him John, which means "gift of God." Zechariah had lost the ability to speak, after being in the Holy of Holies for an extended period of time. All these circumstances pointed to the fact that the child would be special and made the people wonder just what role the child would play. From this, we can see that the people of Christ's time were open to accepting divine phenomena; they were ready to believe. Their achilles heal was their insistent belief that God would act according to their preconceived notions. They expected a great temporal leader who would lead them to material prosperity, not Jesus who would be the Bread of Life and who would be crucified.

LUKE 2:46-48

After three days they found him in the temple, sitting in the midst of the teachers, listening to them and asking them questions... When his parents saw him, they were astonished, and his mother said to him, "Son, why have you done this to us?"

MEDITATIONS & LESSONS

◆   The implication seems to be that in loyalty no one should come before parents. And generally this is true. From a human standpoint, Mary was correct in her reproach. As she saw it, Jesus was not following the fourth Commandment. For his part, Jesus seems to be saying, 'When you were looking for me, why didn't you come here first? You should have known that this is where I would be.' And he reminds his mother that he has another Father, and that there is a higher law than that of Moses.

◆   Everything that Jesus did was related to revealing the Father and saving souls including the souls of Mary and Joseph. So anything done for those purposes was done for Mary and Joseph.

◆   This episode has an obvious application to religious vocations, and indeed, to the life of each individual. We have a heavenly Father, who comes even before our parents and our spouses and our children. There is a higher law than human nature and human wisdom. Anything that helps spread God's Kingdom helps every person in the world, not just the few who are helped directly. "If one member rejoices, we all rejoice."

Luke 3:7

He said to the crowds who came out to be baptized by him, "You brood of vipers! Who warned you to flee from the coming wrath?"

Meditations & Lessons

✦   John the Baptist's greeting was not very cordial. But his question immediately focused the people's attention on God. It is God who is the obvious answer to his question, "Who warned you?" The people may have believed that they came of their own human conviction. However, John made it clear that they had received a special blessing, not received or not accepted by others who failed to come out to see him.

✦   Although the grace to go out to the desert was an act of God's mercy, John preached a God of justice, one who would not forever tolerate man's abusive ways. At some point there must be a time of reckoning, if God has any regard for truth, goodness, and justice.

Luke 3:9-10

"Even now the ax lies at the root of the trees. Therefore every tree that does not produce good fruit will be cut down and thrown into the fire." And the crowds asked him, "What then should we do?"

Meditations & Lessons

✦   The Baptist told them to practice justice and charity toward their neighbor. It it interesting here as in Matthew 25 that neither John the Baptist nor Jesus speak of prayer and worship. They do not speak of the direct relationship between God and man. The fact that the people came into the desert and asked, "What should we do?" signified their faith. But the answer to their question is "love your neighbor as yourself."

✦ Justice and charity are not optional if we wish to be saved.

LUKE 4:22

And all spoke highly of him and were amazed at the gracious words that came from his mouth. They also asked, "Isn't this the son of Joseph?"

MEDITATIONS & LESSONS

✦ The only thing that those in Nazareth had against Jesus was that he was one of their own. Therefore, he could not be better than they. They felt it was "necessary" to bring him to their level.

✦ If we would have any doubts about Jesus being truly man, this passage would be one that would settle the question. His own neighbors had no idea that Jesus was the Christ, so ordinary had been his development in their midst.

LUKE 4:33-34

In the synagogue there was a man with the spirit of an unclean demon, and he cried out in a loud voice, "Ha! What have you to do with us, Jesus of Nazareth? Have you come to destroy us?"

MEDITATIONS & LESSONS

✦ The very presence of God is enough to uncover evil wherever it is. We have often discovered this same fact about ourselves at Mass, in the presence of the Blessed Sacrament, at prayer, in the presence of a holy person. God "appears" to us in so many ways calling us to conversion!

✦ Surely it is God's will to destroy evil, but it is not that easy because we have free will. Evil can be revealed and exposed, but eliminating evil, whether personal or social, demands the exercise of free will, and is not accomplished easily—even when the truth is so evident.

LUKE 4:35-36

Jesus rebuked him and said, "Be quiet! Come out of him!" Then the demon threw the man down in front of them and came out of him without doing him any harm. They were all amazed and said to one another, "What is there about his word?"

MEDITATIONS & LESSONS

✦ At the exercise of Christ's will, at his very word, the evil spirit is overcome. This is a miracle and done only as an example, because ordinarily, it is the exercise of the person's own free will that is required for driving away evil. But Jesus shows us how easily evil can be overcome, if only we use the power we have. After all, moral evil enters in by the same door—free will acceptance of it.

✦ We see examples of this in human nature. By the power of will, illnesses and handicaps are overcome, and games and elections are won. We can do the same with regard to sin, if only we will to do so.

LUKE 5:20-21

When he saw their faith, he said, "As for you, your sins are forgiven." Then the scribes and the Pharisees began to ask themselves,

"Who is this who speaks blasphemies? Who but God alone can forgive sins?"

MEDITATIONS & LESSONS

✦   Although there may have been some confusion at times with regard to the meaning of Christ's words, his words were clear to most of the people most of the time. His words were especially clear to their hearts, if not to their minds. But their hearts were hardened and their minds dimmed. Their question should have been, "If Jesus is not a blasphemer, then who is he?"

✦   More than ever today, human beings are assuming a power that belongs to God only. The scribes and Pharisees were correct in one respect. Only God can forgive sin. Today, many people claim that they confess directly to God. They presume that he has forgiven them. It is a case of the person really forgiving himself. Having deceived themselves, they proceed to receive Holy Communion. Only God can forgive sins and since the coming of Christ, this power has been delegated only to the priest. If there is anything clear in Scripture, it is the conferring upon the Apostles of the power to forgive sins.

LUKE 5:30

The Pharisees and their scribes complained to his disciples, "Why do you eat and drink with tax collectors and sinners?"

MEDITATIONS & LESSONS

✦   We spend most of our time trying to save "the saved." Our sense of mission should be a far stronger. Christ came for sinners. We don't want to exempt anyone from that category, but we are called to make a special missionary effort to those who are clearly recognized in the world as sinners. They should be given a chance as well as ourselves.

✦   It is permitted to associate with the wealthy but not to the extent that one seems to prefer their company to that of the poor. Meetings with the wealthy should be far less frequent than with the poor and/or ordinary people. The purpose of meeting with the wealthy should not be to "extort" money from them, allowing them in that way to save their consciences. The purpose should be to bring them to genuine conversion so that they will give help directly to the poor, on their own, even without receiving credit for it.

Luke 6:1-2

While he was going through a field of grain on the sabbath, his disciples were picking the heads of grain, rubbing them in their hands, and eating them. Some Pharisees said, "Why are you doing what is unlawful on the sabbath?"

Meditations & Lessons

✦   No one followed the Divine Law any more faithfully than Jesus. He also showed respect for Temple authority, but he did make clear a distinction between God's Law and man's law. God's Law gives freedom to man; man's law should do the same, but sometimes it actually shackles human beings. No law should prevent a person from doing that which is in every way good (not just that which seems to be good).

✦   Of course, Jesus also needed opportunities to manifest his divinity. In this case, he showed that he was above man-made laws, superior at least to the Pharisees. Indeed, inasmuch as he clearly knew more than they did about the law, they could have pursued the question to discover that he was, or at least was sent by, the Lawgiver.

LUKE 7:18-19

John's summoned two of his disciples and sent them to the Lord to ask, "Are you the one who is to come, or should we look for another?"

MEDITATIONS & LESSONS

✦   Apparently even John the Baptist was not quite certain that Christ was the Messiah. Then as now, it is extremely difficult to believe the truth, when everyone else disbelieves. The disbelief that greeted Jesus was based on material standards (that the Messiah would be powerful in a worldly way). These false beliefs are impossible to disprove by reason. Jesus made it clear that he was the Messiah by fulfilling the Old Testament prophecy. That, along with the many miracles, was sufficient proof for John.

✦   When we seek an answer from the Lord, we usually discover that the Lord points out the answer which is already staring us in the face, as he did with John. This amounts then to a call to faith: "Fear not, I am with you."

LUKE 7:48-49

He said to her, "Your sins are forgiven." The others at table said to themselves, "Who is this who even forgives sins?"

MEDITATIONS & LESSONS

✦ Although today some would maintain that there is no proof of Christ's divinity in the Gospels, his forgiveness of sins is strong testimony to such a claim. Wherever this is mentioned in the Gospels, the reaction is the same. Only God can forgive sins. And to make clear that he had this power, Christ performed miracles.

LUKE 8:25

"Who then is this, who commands even the winds and the sea, and they obey him?"

MEDITATIONS & LESSONS

✦ If even the winds and the sea are subject to him, how much more should we dependent persons listen to him!

LUKE 8:27-28

When he came ashore a man from the town who was possessed by demons met him...When he saw Jesus, he cried out and fell down before him; in a loud voice he shouted, "What have you to do with me, Jesus, son of the Most High God?"

MEDITATIONS & LESSONS

✦ It is interesting that demons immediately recognized who Jesus was and were immediately subject to him. Was it perhaps that they knew instinctively that they were in the presence of true goodness?

   ✦   On the other hand, as soon as Jesus cast the demon out, the people of the region asked Jesus to leave because they were seized with fear. It is, indeed, strange that they preferred a demon to the Lord.

LUKE 9:52-54

On the way they entered a Samaritan village to prepare for his reception there, but they would not welcome him because the destination of his journey was Jerusalem. When the disciples James and John saw this they asked, "Lord, do you want us to call down fire from heaven to consume them?"

MEDITATIONS & LESSONS

   ✦   Jesus rebuked the two. The response of the Lord could have been for one of two reasons or more likely for both. First, the two disciples lacked an appreciation of his preaching, which was intended to replace the harsh Draconian justice with the law of love. Second, they gave the impression that they were as spiritually powerful as he. They could not expel certain demons because they had not sufficiently prepared with prayer and fasting. How were they so sure that they could get the Father to punish the Samaritans?

   ✦   Believers often act the same way today. We use pious exhortations, when things are going well. We use force and violence, or wish to do so, when people resist us. This is hardly the way of Christ.

LUKE 10:25

There was a scholar of the law who stood up to test him and said, "Teacher, what must I do to inherit eternal life?"

Meditations & Lessons

✦ The scholar knew the answer: "You shall love the Lord your God with all your heart, with all your being, with all your strength, and with all your mind, and your neighbor as yourself." He was asking to see whether or not Christ would confirm or challenge the Old Testament. It was a valid question. It was also a point that apparently was not well understood in those days. Materialism had crept in.

✦ A more technical, theological answer today would also make clear that it is impossible to love God and neighbor without God's grace. Eternal life, like human life and the means to attain it, are all gifts of God, perfectly free to give or not to give on his part.

LUKE 10:29

But because he wished to justify himself, he said to Jesus, "And who is my neighbor?"

Meditations & Lessons

✦ Jesus answered this question with the story of the Good Samaritan. In effect, he said that everyone is our neighbor.

✦ Here is another case of Jesus using a question, which had not been asked with the highest of intentions, to instruct us on a very important issue.

LUKE 10:40

Martha, burdened with much serving came to him and said, "Lord, do you not care that my sister has left me by myself to do the serving?"

MEDITATIONS & LESSONS

✦ Mary had not chosen to abandon Martha; she had made the much more positive choice to adore the Lord. Contemplatives cannot get along very well without the support of people who lead active rather than contemplative lives. The working person has a value in society. But to say that the contemplative has chosen the better part is not to say that other persons have made a poor choice. It seems clear elsewhere that Christ very much respected Martha's practical role as head of the household.

✦ Comparisons can be odious. They may serve as a means of clarifying an explanation, but every human being should appreciate that he is nothing. Remember, man, that you are dust and unto dust you shall return—even the most powerful and wealthy. The only person, with whom we are to compare ourselves, is God. In perfection, we come in a woeful last. In regard to our human life, certainly Christ was asked to endure much more than we. Comparing ourselves with other human beings is usually self-defeating. Most often it produces pride, but sometimes it can develop an unwarranted loss of confidence because we lose sight of the fact that despite our deficiencies, God loves us.

LUKE 12:37-41

"Blessed are those servants whom the master finds vigilant on his arrival...You also must be prepared, for at an hour you do not expect, the Son of Man will come." Then Peter said, "Lord, is this parable meant for us or for everyone?"

MEDITATIONS & LESSONS

✦ The direct answer to the question is clear. Although the parable is for all, the teaching of Jesus applies in a special way to the Apostles. Because they have received more from the Father, more will be demanded of them. It will be easier to excuse the shortcomings of others, but the Apostles are to be held to the ideal, to perfection.

✦ The Apostles must be perfect servants. They must do their work whether the Master knows of it or not. They must not only serve the Master, they must serve their fellow servants.

✦ The whole parable makes clear, however, that because the Apostles have received more than others, and due to the excellence of their service, they will have a certain hierarchical rank of leadership, which comes from God's grace of appointment and from the moral suasion of their example.

LUKE 13:23

"Lord, will only a few people be saved?"

MEDITATIONS & LESSONS

✦ Jesus does not answer the question directly, but he makes it very clear that not everyone will be saved.

✦ We should not be interested so much in what God is going to do for us, but what we are going to do for God. If we make our best effort to live exactly as God wants us to live, we have nothing to worry about. If we try for anything less than that, we can find ourselves in trouble. So our question should not imply that we are asking how little we can do and still be saved. We should be striving to do our utmost because salvation is never guaranteed, especially to those who are looking for an "easy out".

LUKE 18:18

"Good teacher, what must I do to inherit eternal life?"

MEDITATIONS & LESSONS

✦   The Ten Commandments are the basic minimum. If we are keeping them, we have a good chance. But for greater certitude, the practice of virtue is necessary. We must not only do the minimum; but also we must practice charity. We must not only be just in our dealings, but we must be loving towards God and others, too. If our lives are built on love, heaven will surely be ours.

✦   In an act of love Jesus invites the man to sell all that he has, give it to the poor, and "come follow me". Jesus, of course, wants all to follow him, but, as in this case, there are some whom he invites into a special relationship. Too often, like the man in the Gospel, we think about what we must give up to follow Jesus rather than focusing on what we get by following him.

LUKE 18:26

"Then who can be saved?"

MEDITATIONS & LESSONS

✦   Many people in the world are willing to do the minimum. Many are willing to practice justice, but not nearly as many are willing to be charitable, to give to others what they have no right to, what they have not worked for.

✦ We often confuse charity and justice. We rarely exercise charity to the full by depriving ourselves of something so that we can give it to another person who has no claim upon us. When we give, we usually give from our surplus. We do it, not necessarily because we see the other person's need, but in order to make ourselves feel good.

✦ God is good and merciful. As many as can be saved will be saved.

LUKE 20:22

"Is it lawful for us to pay tribute to Caesar or not?"

MEDITATIONS & LESSONS

✦ Civil order is necessary for peace and prosperity. We cannot live in anarchy and have any semblance of peace or the freedom to pursue happiness. At the same time, the whole context of the Gospel seems to indicate that Jesus is not especially enthusiastic for Caesar. Government is not evil in itself, and it is necessary. Yet, history is replete with examples of human beings abusing their power over others.

✦ Although it is lawful to give tribute to Caesar, it is the duty of government to work for the common good. Government should be a servant, not a master. If it should turn into a master, as was the case with the Romans, taxes will be paid grudgingly and perhaps at some time, one would be justified in refusing to pay.

LUKE 20:33

"Now at the resurrection whose wife will that woman be?"

Meditations & Lessons

✦   The Sadducees who asked this question did not believe in the resurrection. Perhaps that was because of the way they looked at the world. Indeed, in the terms of this world, It is difficult to believe in the resurrection of the body and immortality. If an after-life involves nothing better than the present life, it would seem foolish to believe in it.

✦   The best reason for believing in immortality is God's Word, but apart from that, the best logical reason for such belief is the suffering and injustice of this world. We know that God is good and that injustice and suffering would not be permitted unless it was for a greater good.

✦   The ultimate reason for marriage in this world is so that we can more readily find salvation by working to that end with a partner. Priests and religious respect the vocation of marriage, but they believe that God calls them to have him alone as their most intimate partner as they journey through life. Since the after-life consists in the direct vision of God and union with him, a person no longer needs the help of another. The goal has been attained, safe harbor reached, help is no longer needed. So, although spouses may be present to one another some way in heaven, the need of the same type of union is no longer present.

Luke 21:5-7

While some people were speaking about how the temple was adorned ...he said, "All that you see here—the days will come when there will not be left a stone upon another stone that will not be thrown down." Then they asked him, "Teacher, when will this happen? And what sign will there be when all these things are about to happen?"

Meditations & Lessons

✦   The principal concern of the Apostles—about the destruction of Jerusalem—seems to be clearly answered in verse 20. "When you see Jerusalem surrounded by armies, know that its desolation is at hand." The end of the world is discussed in verses 25-28 — "There will be signs in the sun, the moon, and the stars, and on earth, nations will be in dismay ..."— seems to be presaged by elements of the universe losing the pattern, in which they presently are fixed.

✦   Through the course of history, there are always human and natural disasters and persecutions. Simply because these things occur does not mean that the end is at hand. They are to be expected, and, indeed, they provide marvelous opportunities to proclaim the faith. We have one of those opportunities now. There are even attacks upon the faith from within the Church. If we look upon defense of the faith as a romantic adventure (the Apostles, St. Thomas More, etc.), their times were no more wonderful than ours in this regard.

Luke 22:8-9

He sent out Peter and John, instructing them, "Go and make preparations for us to eat the Passover." They asked him, "Where do you want us to make the preparations?"

Meditations & Lessons

✦   We should be constantly available to do what the Lord wants, in the manner he wants, when he wants. In this case, it is evident that the Lord does have a way, that his way is good, and that we often (always!) learn that his is far better than anything we could plan or imagine.

LUKE 22:48-49

He went up to Jesus to kiss him. Jesus said to him, "Judas, are you betraying the Son of Man with a kiss?" His disciples realized what was about to happen, and they asked, "Lord, shall we strike with the sword?"

MEDITATIONS & LESSONS

+ In this case, even the Lord found it difficult to make himself clear in his teaching. He had used "sword" as a figure of speech on several occasions, but he had never encouraged the Apostles to violence. Still, just as he had taken time to explain certain simple parables, apparently there were other matters that did not come across clearly. In preaching and teaching, one cannot be too careful.

+ A case for self defense is made, but a good case can also be made for pacifism in the Gospels. This is not a strong text in regard to pacifism, but it does remind us that Jesus' approach was one of peace and love. Have we misunderstood him? Has our philosophy and theology been too favorable to self-defense, such as justified war? Should we lean more to pacifism?

LUKE 22:63-64

The men who held Jesus in custody were ridiculing him and beating him. They blindfolded him and questioned him, saying, "Prophesy! Who is it that struck you?"

MEDITATIONS & LESSONS

+ As if it makes any difference! A sinful act is not made sinful by discovery, but by the intention of the one who commits the act. And in the story of Jesus, it does not matter so much as to which person struck the blow because, in a very true sense, it was struck by each one of us, who has sinned against the Lord. So Jesus does not answer.

LUKE 22:67-70

They said, "If you are the Messiah, tell us," but he replied to them, "If I tell you, you will not believe, and if I question, you will not respond. But from this time on the Son of Man will be seated at the right hand of the power of God." They all asked, "Are you then the Son of God?"

MEDITATIONS & LESSONS

✦ Christ did not go around claiming that he was the Messiah, because many in that time were doing so. Actions speak much louder than words. If he had proclaimed himself as Messiah, it would have been even more difficult for the people to take him seriously because of the many false prophets. So he took the other approach. By so doing, he made the people believe in their hearts—even the scribes and Pharisees—that he was indeed an extraordinary person who, if accepted, would turn their way of life upside down. Therefore, they charged him with something that he had not said openly—you are making yourself out to be the Son of God—and they had him put to death for blasphemy.

LUKE 22:71

Then they said, "What further need have we for testimony?"

Meditations & Lessons

✦   Christ still refused to make a confession of his divinity. "If I tell you, you will not believe." There was no reason to proclaim his divinity outright, because he would not be given a chance to validate the claim. They had already made up their minds that he was an impostor, guilty of blasphemy. An admission of divinity at this point would have only further confirmed them in their error, so he did not respond directly. Still, they claimed that he had "confessed."

Luke 23:3

Pilate asked him, "Are you the king of the Jews?"

Meditations & Lessons

✦   This question and response are very much like the previous one. Pilate knew that Jesus was not claiming to be king, in the ordinary sense of the term, "king" (he had no troops, nor was he threatening an armed rebellion), but Pilate was hardly prepared to accept the spiritual answer that Jesus could give. So again, Jesus says in effect, "Draw your own conclusions. Believe what you will. If you want a real explanation, I'm ready to give it to you. But if your question is only perfunctory and you're going to do what the crowd wants anyway, there is no sense in my wasting my breath."

Luke 23:20-22

Again Pilate addressed them, still wishing to release Jesus, but they continued their shouting, "Crucify him! Crucify him!" Pilate addressed them a third time, "What evil has this man done?"

MEDITATIONS & LESSONS

✦ Even at the very end, no one could convict Christ of sin or crime. In the Roman Law there had to be a reason, a crime, in order to convict, and there was none. So, in effect, Christ was put to death for claiming to be king of the Jews (blasphemy in the Jewish Law), which in no way had been proven. He had no troops; he had not fomented rebellion; he was unarmed.

✦ The same type of "fever" can arise with regard to accusations made against a priest. It is one thing to accuse a priest of some kind of misconduct in a parish, but quite another to convict him once both sides have been heard and once other people in the parish are heard. This is especially dangerous where there is a one-man jury or judge, as is the case when complaints come directly to the Bishop or through the Personnel Board. So often much of what is said is second hand.

LUKE 23:39

Now one of the criminals hanging there reviled Jesus, saying, "Are you not the Messiah?"

MEDITATIONS & LESSONS

✦ Even the thief recognized that Jesus, through his actions, had laid claim to being the Messiah, he had raised people from the dead and done other remarkable feats. But he was being put to death for these "crimes" because the Jewish people believed that he was a charlatan of some kind, rather than the Christ. So the cynical thief took the part of the crowd.

Luke 23:40

The other, however, rebuking him, said in reply, "Have you no fear of God, for you are subject to the same condemnation?"

Meditations & Lessons

✦　The good thief had heard all the stories about Jesus too—so they were common knowledge—but he wasn't so sure of Jesus' "guilt or innocence". Better to play it safe. Convicted criminals should be the last to condemn a fellow "criminal" anyway. "Judge not, lest you be judged."

Luke 24:2-5

They found the stone rolled away from the tomb; but when they entered, they did not find the body of the Lord Jesus. While they were puzzling over this, behold, two men in dazzling garments appeared to them. They were terrified and bowed their faces to the ground. They said to them, "Why do you seek the living one among the dead?"

Meditations & Lessons

✦　Although the women had great love and loyalty for Christ, apparently their faith was still uncertain, or they still did not realize fully who Jesus was. The more basic question was whether or not they believed Jesus to be divine. If so, "Why do you seek the living among the dead?"

LUKE 24:18

"Are you the only visitor to Jerusalem who does not know of the things that have taken place there in these days?"

MEDITATIONS & LESSONS

✦   The question which Cleopas asked of the resurrected Jesus is full of unintentional irony. Jesus was indeed the only one who truly understood the events of the last few days.

✦   From the question, it would seem that Jesus was well known, that his trial and execution gained notoriety, that there were some unusual aspects to it all that stirred the people, and yet no one rose in his defense.

✦   It is possible that the Disciples were being subjective and thought more people were aware of what had happened than in fact did. However, their view was probably valid. The remarkable conversions at Pentecost would seem to bear this out.

✦   Christianity has spread so widely throughout the world that we might ask the same question today. And yet there are many who have never heard of Jesus, or who have heard of him, but have never rallied to his cause. Rather than responding impatiently, we should react like a good teacher, taking advantage of the question raised in society to explain over and over again the life and teachings of the Lord, as Pope John Paul II has done on his visits to countries around the world.

LUKE 24:30-32

And it happened that, while he was with them at table, he took bread, said the blessing, broke it, and gave it to them. With that their eyes were opened and they recognized him, but he vanished from their sight. Then they said to each other, "Were not our hearts burning [within us] while he spoke to us on the way and opened the scriptures to us?"

MEDITATIONS & LESSONS

✦   Although this could have been expressing embarrassment at not having recognized Jesus, it is more likely that in recalling how they felt when they met Jesus on the road, they were confirming that somehow they were aware of his presence, even if that awareness did not reach the conscious level. The truth both illuminated their intellects and made them desire to know more. At the same time, they wanted to tell others about God's revelation and its meaning for our lives.

✦   We should be ready to teach anyone anywhere in the same way that Jesus did. We should try to set souls on fire not by short-lived emotion, but with the long-burning flame of truth.

CHAPTER EIGHT

Questions Others Asked in the Gospel of John

In some ways, John's Gospel is the most intimate and personal of the four Gospels. It is in this Gospel that we see John leaning his head on Jesus' chest and asking which of the Apostles would betray him. We seem to get a first hand, eye witness account of Peter's betrayal. This is also the Gospel which recounts the story of the woman at the well. Since, the Disciples had left Jesus alone, he must have recounted what happened when they were gone at least to John or perhaps to all of the Apostles.

JOHN 1:19-22

When the Jews from Jerusalem sent priests and Levites [to him] to ask him, "Who are you?...What are you then? Are you Elijah?... Are you the Prophet?...Who are you, so we can give an answer to those who sent us? What do you have to say for yourself?"

Meditations & Lessons

✦   John the Baptist knows who he is and what his role is. He immediately declared, "I am not the Messiah."

✦   We would probably give our name and address and next of kin as an answer. To identify himself, John the Baptist gives his purpose in life. That is an excellent means of self-identification. My answer today should be, "I am a priest, trying to bring God's message of salvation to all people, especially those of my diocese." Name, address and next of kin would help very little in identifying me.

✦   Actually, our own answer should be very much the same as that of the Baptist. "I am 'the voice of one crying out in the desert, make straight the way of the Lord.' " When it comes to the message of Christ, we are like a voice in the desert. Those who say they are interested, really are not that interested, when the chips are down. For example, few pursue family devotion, lives of prayer, and scripture studies, or show concern for the less fortunate. Those with deep commitment to these values are pitifully few.

✦   The message is to follow in the way, the truth and the life of Jesus Christ. That, too, is a straight path. There are no twists and turns to accommodate error, sinful pleasure, no vacation from the Christian life. Today some moralists claim that individual actions are of no account as long as our overall orientation is directed to God! That is hardly in keeping with John's message, hardly the message that we should be preaching.

John 1:25

They asked him, "Why then do you baptize if you are not the Messiah or Elijah or the Prophet?"

Meditations & Lessons

✦ Baptism is an initiation rite. It was performed as a sign that a person had accepted a certain life style and was going to live in accordance with that life. John was baptizing with this intention, but in anticipation of the message of Christ, which was yet to come. His message was to repent and be converted to God so that they would be prepared for the Word, when he would shortly appear.

✦ Since we are baptized as infants, it is sometimes difficult to appreciate the meaning of baptism. We need to reflect more upon it, or at least to recognize that reception of every sacrament—including the Eucharist—is a renewal of our baptismal commitment. How can we receive Communion without a solemn vow to convert ourselves more fully to God and to walk in his straight path?

John 1:38

They said to him, "Rabbi...where are you staying?"

Meditations & Lessons

✦ The question would seem to mean, what kind of a life do you live? After all, the Disciples knew where John lived, but it would seem that his style of life and his message were the attraction that drew them. If John thought highly of Jesus, surely he would be living in similar circumstances. "The Son of Man has nowhere to lay his head."

✦ If we want to know what the Christ-life is all about, we must try it. Like golf or some other sport, talking about the techniques will get us nowhere. Trying the life may be frustrating, too, but it will be productive.

✦ A monk, experiencing spiritual dryness, was told by his confessor to keep two buckets in his room. He was to take one of them to the well each day (the same one), fill it with water, pour the water back into the well, and return the bucket to his room. A month later he told the confessor that the buckets were no help. The confessor showed surprise and asked what the buckets looked like. "Both just sit there empty and one is full of cobwebs." "Ah, that's the point, my son," replied the confessor, "keep trying to pray. Your efforts may seem fruitless, your soul empty, but as a matter of fact, its state is like the clean, clear bucket rather than like the one full of cobwebs."

John 1:45-46

Philip found Nathaniel and told him, "We have found the one about whom Moses wrote in the law, and also the prophets, Jesus, son of Joseph, from Nazareth." But Nathaniel said to him, "Can anything good come from Nazareth?"

Meditations & Lessons

✦   Prejudice is always a problem for us. Our own experiences as well as the teaching and example of others, predispose our thinking of others. Our predispositions are often so ingrained that we can not simply forget them. Yet each human being has a unique dignity which requires us not to prejudge him. If Nathaniel had not overcome his prejudice at least to this degree, he would never have become a follower of Christ.

✦   We may be missing opportunities to meet wonderful people due to our prejudices about race, color, nationality, religion or other things.

✦   Good can came out of anything. The axiom that "God always brings some good out of evil"—otherwise he could not permit evil—is quite true. We know that much spiritual good often develops from sickness, which is a physical evil. Even moral evil is oftentimes the soil from which great spiritual good springs, as is the case with St. Augustine, and leads others to prayer.

JOHN 1:47-48

Jesus saw Nathaniel coming toward him and said of him, "Here is a true Israelite. There is no duplicity in him." Nathaniel said to him, "How do you know me?"

MEDITATIONS & LESSONS

✦ God knows all about all of us—every thought, word and deed. In such circumstances, it is amazing that any believer should ever sin. Sin is a sign that we have forgotten God—excluded him from our thoughts. So we must be not only believers, but prayers as well—people who frequently have the Lord on our minds. Then, sin is next to impossible.

✦ Another sign that Christ is God, or at least someone sent by God, is that he had special knowledge that he did not receive from other human beings.

✦ God is concerned for everyone, no matter who we are, what our circumstances are. He came to save us even when we were still sinners. There is never any excuse for discouragement. He is very much aware of us; all we need to do is go to him.

JOHN 2:14-18

He found in the temple area those who sold oxen, sheep, and doves, as well as the money-changers seated there. He made a whip out of cords and drove them all out of the temple area, with the sheep and oxen, and spilled the coins of the money-changers and overturned their tables, and to those who sold doves, he said, "Take these out of here, and stop making my Father's house a marketplace." At this the Jews answered and said to him, "What sign can you show us for doing this?"

MEDITATIONS & LESSONS

✦   The fact that Jesus came right back with an answer—"Destroy this temple and in three days I will raise it up."—even though they could not understand it, should have been a sign to the Jews that they should think over what he had said and done.

✦   The sign, of course, was to be the Resurrection. Again, it would be impossible to understand at this time, but the Lord's answer should have led to more questions.

✦   The real temple, the indestructible temple, is the Temple of the Holy Spirit, who dwelled within Christ and who dwells within us. If we are faithful to the Holy Spirit, we too will be "rebuilt" very quickly after death, no matter how we may be brought to that moment, for example, cancer, fire, accident, etc.

JOHN 2:20

The Jews said, "This temple has been under construction for forty-six years, and you will raise it up in three days?"

MEDITATIONS & LESSONS

✦   The answer, of course, was "yes," but they were speaking of altogether different temples. It would be easier to replace bricks and mortar than to raise oneself from the dead—that had never been done before.

✦ We can devote a lifetime to something that seems to be important but it means nothing when compared to the will of God. The building of the temple, good though it was, is such a case. Whole lifetimes were spent on its construction, while the spiritual lives of the builders were crumbling. "What does it profit a man...?" Of what profit are our worldly accomplishments to ourselves?

JOHN 3:3-4

Jesus answered and said to him, "Amen, amen, I say to you, no one can see the kingdom of God without being born from above." Nicodemus said to him, "How can a person once grown old be born again? Surely he cannot reenter his mother's womb and be born again, can he?"

MEDITATIONS & LESSONS

✦ The term that Jesus was using for "birth" must have been so forceful and real that even an educated man like Nicodemus missed the point. Jesus was speaking about a spiritual rebirth, but he was so intent on making it clear that he was not merely using symbolism but was speaking of a spiritual reality that would take place, that Nicodemus did not at first understand his meaning.

JOHN 3:9

Nicodemus answered and said to him, "How can this happen?"

Meditations & Lessons

✦   This is the same question asked by Mary in Luke 1:34. It is not a case of Nicodemus not accepting what Jesus says, but rather expressing wonder as to how such a spiritual reality (the coming of the Holy Spirit within a person) can be possible. He does not understand but he is ready to believe because of his faith in Christ.

✦   Of course, as in the case of Mary, anything is possible to God. This will be accomplished by the power of the Holy Spirit. "The Spirit breathes where he wills."

John 4:7-9

A woman of Samaria came to draw water. Jesus said to her, "Give me a drink."... The Samaritan woman said to him, "How can you, a Jew, ask me, a Samaritan woman, for a drink?"

Meditations & Lessons

✦   Jews and Samaritans had nothing to do with one another. The woman had learned the man-made "law" of hatred which existed between Jews and Samaritans. In her mind, this took precedence over the God-given laws of human decency. The right to ask for water and the obligation to give water, which was so basic an obligation in the area, meant nothing in comparison to the obligations of hatred.

✦   Why did Jesus ask? He was trying to break down man-made prejudices (against religion, race, sex, and nationality) in favor of the innate laws of God. God's ways can easily be discovered by even the most simple person, if only he is freed from the slavery which is caused by the burdens that so-called wise men have placed upon him.

John 4:10-12

Jesus answered and said to her, "If you knew the gift of God and who is saying to you, 'Give me a drink,' you would have asked him and he would have given you living water." [The woman] said to him, "Sir, you do not even have a bucket and the cistern is deep; where then can you get this living water? Are you greater than our father Jacob, who gave us this cistern and drank from it himself with his children and his flocks?"

Meditations & Lessons

✦ Either out of politeness or curiosity, most people are willing to give us a hearing if we show concern for them when we approach them. It is always hard to know when interest or curiosity will give way to faith because faith is not of man's making but a gift of God. Our part is to evangelize, catechize, do all the basics like knocking on doors. Bringing forth fruit is God's work.

✦ The woman was a believer; she had faith in Jacob. Like the woman, most people are ready to believe. Life on earth prompts people to hope for something better. It is up to us to make our message credible. We do that in many ways but especially by the example of our own lives. The greatest sign of credibility is that we live what we preach and that this produces peace and joy in our lives.

John 4:28-29

The woman left her water jar and went into the town and said to the people, "Come and see a man who told me everything I have done. Could he possibly be the Messiah?"

Meditations & Lessons

✦   It was obvious that the woman recognized the qualities of the Messiah in Jesus, and, indeed, Jesus identified himself to her as Messiah. Even so, she had questions. Faith is a gift of God. Good will is required on our part, but even that does not "demand" of God the gift of faith. It may be the Christ, but is it? The woman had difficulty in making that "leap of faith".

✦   The woman goes to others for moral support. Since faith is acceptance of truths that we cannot always see or prove, we shall always be in need of a religious community to strengthen our faith and to enable us to deal with doubts. Ordinarily speaking, there are just too many worldly forces for a person of faith to deal with by himself.

John 4:31-33

Meanwhile, the disciples urged him, "Rabbi, eat." But he said to them, "I have food to eat of which you do not know. So the disciples said to one another, "Could someone have brought him something to eat?"

Meditations & Lessons

✦   Apparently the incident took place early in the public ministry of Christ. The Apostles seemed to be as mystified as Nicodemus had been. They had no conception of the supernatural powers of the Messiah. Even though they could be quite certain that he had no food, their minds still turned to natural explanations rather than supernatural ones.

John 6:8-9

One of his disciples, Andrew, the brother of Simon Peter, said to him, "There is a boy here who has five barley loaves and two fish; but what good are these for so many?"

Meditations & Lessons

✦ The same could hold true for priests and religious today. Especially as our numbers dwindle and as we look at a worse situation in other countries, we could ask the same question. But if we give ourselves generously into the hands of the Lord, he can work wonders with us. On the other hand, if we allow ourselves to dry up and to go stale and do not offer ourselves to the Lord, he has little or nothing to work with. Then, we are indeed too little—not in numbers but in generosity—to have any effect.

John 6:24-25

When the crowds saw that neither Jesus nor his disciples were there, they themselves got into boats and came to Capernaum looking for Jesus. And when they found him across the sea, they said to him, "Rabbi, when did you get here?"

Meditations & Lessons

✦ Even after the miracle of the loaves and fishes, the people thought that Jesus escaped them only by some form of human trickery— either he left at an earlier time or he took a faster boat. Down deep, they knew that they were wrong, but they asked the question anyway. This is a good sign that the crowd was not easily convinced of miracles, as some modern critics would have it.

John 6:26-28

Jesus answered them and said, "Amen, amen, I say to you, you are looking for me not because you saw signs but because you ate the loaves and were filled. Do not work for food that perishes but for the food that endures for eternal life, which the Son of Man will give you. For on him the Father, God, has set his seal. So they said to him, "What can we do to accomplish the works of God?"

Meditations & Lessons

+ The people prided themselves on the fact that they kept the law rigorously. What else could be required of them? If Jesus' answer was something other than the law, it would probably contravene the law. So this was a safe question. They knew what the works of God were, and they were trying to accomplish them.

+ Christ could have cast the gauntlet of love right then and there, explaining that they were not keeping the spirit of the law. But that was a no-win argument. Instead, he pointed to his own person. A true prophet does not destroy the law but leads to a greater fulfillment of the law. Accept him as a prophet and there is no need for argument.

+ In our own day the Lord responds in similar fashion. "I'm not going to get into an argument with you concerning your interpretations of the Gospel. Just accept that the Holy Father is the Vicar of Jesus Christ on earth and what further need have we of argument?"

JOHN 6:29-30

Jesus answered and said to them, "This is the work of God, that you believe in the one he sent." So they said to him, "What sign can you do, that we may see and believe in you? What can you do?"

MEDITATIONS & LESSONS

+ Although Christ spoke in the simplest form possible (parables) and gave the people countless miracles as the strongest possible proof of his divine mission, they would not accept either. They always had need of some further proof. For us, as for the Jews, we should realize that faith is a gift of God and not the result of a reasoning process.

+ One could hardly come up with a greater miracle than that of the loaves and fishes, but they did—the manna in the desert. Still, they were playing right into the hands of the Lord; he had a greater bread miracle to reveal to them. The Lord was one step ahead of them with each of their questions. But when he finally promised them what they asked for, they rejected it as preposterous. They simply were not disposed to believe.

+ Here, again, is a case where in response to questioning, he reveals a great mystery. If we ask, we will receive the answers we need.

JOHN 6:41-42

The Jews murmured about him because he said, "I am the bread that came down from heaven," and they said, "Is this not Jesus, the son of Joseph? Do we not know his father and mother? Then how can he say, 'I have come down from heaven?'"

MEDITATIONS & LESSONS

✦   There was no question whatever in the minds of the Jews that Christ was truly man in every sense of the word. We who have been brought up with an emphasis on his divinity sometimes have a difficulty accepting his complete humanity. We might reflect more on passages such as this one.

✦   Through our parents we receive so much of what we are! A good tree can only bear good fruit. By their fruits you will know them.

✦   The Jews knew Jesus' origins, so they knew he was human. But it became clear to them that Christ was claiming divinity. The question was whether or not they would accept him as he is. Everyone comes from heaven, in the sense that God creates each person; clearly they were not confused on that score; they knew what Christ was saying.

JOHN 6:52

The Jews quarreled among themselves, saying, "How can this man give us [his] flesh to eat?"

MEDITATIONS & LESSONS

✦   Jesus' answer certainly did seem to be incredible. But then, the Jews were asking for something "incredible"—a divine sign, a sign from heaven, a miracle. If they were sincere about what they were asking, there should have been some indication on their part that they were ready or willing to believe.

✦   Jesus answered every question. Frequently, he anticipated the questioners and led them to ask other questions. But he always answered. Even on those occasions when he spoke no words (for example, before

Herod and Pilate), his silence spoke more eloquently than words ever could speak.

JOHN 6:60

Then many of his disciples who were listening said, "This saying is hard; who can accept it?"

MEDITATIONS & LESSONS

✦   There is no question that Christ's words were a "hard saying." No one can accept the statement on human grounds. Faith in the person speaking is the only trustworthy means of believing. If Christ is God, belief still remains difficult, but all things are possible to God. This is why it can be said that the principal question for us to answer is, "But who do you say I am?" And why Christ states that faith is a gift of the Father (verse 65).

JOHN 6:66-68

As a result of this, many of his disciples returned to their former way of life and no longer accompanied him. Jesus then said to the Twelve, "Do you also want to leave?" Simon Peter answered him, "Master, to whom shall we go?"

MEDITATIONS & LESSONS

✦   Once we commit ourselves to Christ, there is nowhere else to go. Notice that when Catholics give up their faith, they rarely join another Church, or if they do, it is usually for social reasons. They seem to sense that they have had the best that religion can offer in the Catholic faith and that, if Catholicism cannot meet their expectations, nothing will.

 ✦   Peter reduces the test to one of personality, which is all that can be done in the face of mystery. The question is not so much what we think of Jesus' statements, but what we think of Jesus himself. If we believe him to be a man only, we walk away. If we believe him to be God, there is nothing to do but accept his word no matter what he says.

 ✦   This is another reason for insisting on permanency of commitment in the Church. Once we have put our hand to the plow, accepted a ministry to which God has called us, where else is there to go? There's nowhere else to go, but down. It is something else entirely if one did not have a divine vocation in the first place, but that is not what priests and sisters have been saying. The priest is a priest forever, so it would seem that he will be judged (not unmercifully) on what he has done as a priest, even though married.

JOHN 7:11

The Jews were looking for him at the feast and saying, "Where is he?"

MEDITATIONS & LESSONS

 ✦   Many looked upon Christ as a performer. He was not appreciated as much for the way, the truth, and the life that he had to preach, but for his entertainment value. He was sensational; he was sure to cause excitement.

 ✦   Neither the Apostles nor the crowds could understand why Jesus did not push himself more into the limelight. Where was he? He was at the same place that he had been for thirty years, living a life of holiness. His primary desire was to do his Father's will.

John 7:14-15

When the feast was already half over, Jesus went up into the temple area and began to teach. The Jews were amazed and said, "How does he know scripture without having studied?"

Meditations & Lessons

✦ The response of Jesus—"My teaching is not my own but is from the one who sent me"—would seem to be contrary to the modern thesis that Jesus gained all his knowledge gradually and did not understand that he was God. Of course, the Gospels were written after the Resurrection, but the authors were still trying to portray Jesus as he really was and as he really appeared on earth. The knowledge that Jesus had from the Father must have been infused or a result of the Beatific Vision; it does not seem that Jesus gained this knowledge in the way others gain knowledge. Normally one needs to study in order to gain knowledge.

✦ The Jews respected Jesus as having great learning, great wisdom, as being extraordinary. Who has ever heard anything like this? He is one speaking with authority.

✦ Once again the Jews were given a sign of divinity, but they could not bring themselves to acknowledge it. He is still just a man, even though he possesses extraordinary language and has never studied.

John 7:19-20

"Did not Moses give you the law? Yet none of you keeps the law. Why are you trying to kill me?" The crowd answered, "You are possessed! Who is trying to kill you?"

Meditations & Lessons

✦　　Some of the people probably could not see what was coming. However, their continual baiting of Christ and their refusal to listen was bound to lead to more serious accusations. At the time, they might have had no intention of killing Jesus, but they were certainly trying to overcome him, defeat him, refute him in every way possible.

✦　　Here is an example of an attempt to demonize a foe. They tried to make Jesus a devil because they would not have to listen to a devil.

John 7:25

Some of the inhabitants of Jerusalem said, "Is he not the one they are trying to kill?"

Meditations & Lessons

✦　　This question makes clear that the leaders of the Jews were trying to put Christ to death. It was an open secret. It is equally clear that Jesus had already been tried and convicted on the streets. The judgment of his guilt had already been made; he would be given no formal trial, only a mock trial; it would not be objective and unprejudiced.

John 7:26

"Could the authorities have realized that he is the Messiah?"

Meditations & Lessons

✦　　The authorities were simply asking themselves the wrong questions. They were trying to discover whether Jesus was claiming divine powers. However, they were not raising the question as to whether these signs proved him to be the Messiah. They were deliberately blinding themselves to that question. They did not really want the Messiah to come in their time because they would lose their power. So automatically, one who claimed divine power was guilty of blasphemy.

✦ The authorities had said plenty to Jesus. Why they did not challenge him at this time was uncertain. Perhaps they were hoping that he would just go away. Perhaps they were uncertain of their ground. More likely, they had made up their minds to kill him, and they were busy making their case and looking for the right opportunity.

JOHN 7:31

But many of the crowd began to believe in him, and said, "When the Messiah comes, will he perform more signs than this man has done?"

MEDITATIONS & LESSONS

✦ We do need signs that someone claiming to be the Messiah is truly he. Christ told the Jews that he would give no more signs, but this verse indicates that he had already given them more than enough signs. Moreover, he did promise to give them the sign of signs, the Resurrection, in fulfillment of prophecy—his own and that of the Old Testament.

✦ Why don't we receive more signs? The answer is that we have the sign of signs—the life, the teachings, and the Resurrection of Christ, attested for two thousand years by the lives of the saints and the deaths of martyrs.

✦   The perfection of Christ's life—no one could convict him of sin—and the proven truth of his teaching as preserved in the Church, despite the disruptions of centuries, are the best signs that we have to believe today.

✦   The question is like the one I ask myself in response to doubts of faith. If there is no God, what then? His existence seems to be the only reasonable explanation of life. And if there is a God, everything of our faith falls into place—the Trinity, the Incarnation, and the Church.

John 7:35-36

So the Jews said to one another, "Where is he going that we will not find him?...What is the meaning of his saying, 'You will look for me and not find [me], and where I am you cannot come'?"

Meditations & Lessons

✦   It would seem obvious that Jesus saw his life as a continuum, that it began before the incarnation and would continue after his death and resurrection in a place where non-believers and sinners cannot enter. He would return to his home, a place where they had never been and would never be admitted.

✦   Now—on earth—is the time to seek, find, accept, embrace Christ, if we wish to be with him where he has gone. To delay is to lose the opportunity. And yet, this is what we do; we seek ourselves, our own pleasure, our own satisfaction, and our own will until often it is too late.

✦   The Pharisees were confident that, together with the Roman soldiers, there was no way on earth for anyone to escape them. Where could he go? They were to find out that the powers of this world are no match for divine power, and as religious leaders, they above all should have appreciated that fact, and they should have been preaching and acting in accordance with it.

John 7:40-42

Some in the crowd who heard these words...said, "This is the Messiah." But others said, "The Messiah will not come from Galilee, will he? Does not scripture say that the Messiah will be of David's family and come from Bethlehem, the village where David lived?"

Meditations & Lessons

✦   It would seem that the genealogy of the Christ was no great secret. When Herod inquired, the answer came directly from his advisors; in this case, all the people seem to have a good understanding of his lineage. So there is no question that Jesus fulfilled this well-known prophecy, which would be another sign of his divinity or at least give cause for the people to study his claims most seriously.

John 7:43-45

So a division occurred in the crowd because of him. Some of them even wanted to arrest him, but no one laid hands on him. So the guards went to the chief priests and Pharisees, who asked them, "Why did you not bring him?"

Meditations & Lessons

✦   Why did they not take charge of the arrest themselves? They wanted others "to do the dirty work". The whole project could backfire on them because the people were divided. The Pharisees needed a possible scapegoat; they were concerned for their own popularity; they did not wish to face in an open forum a person who spoke with authority.

✦   We are not sure what position the officers were taking, but it seems certain that they were impressed—either by his innocence or the power of his appeal to the people or a combination of several things. In any instance, they saw no possibility in the circumstances of arresting him, and if that be the case, far less chance of convicting him in an honest trial.

John 7:46-48

The guards answered, "Never before has anyone spoken like this one." So the Pharisees answered them, "Have you also been deceived? Have any of the authorities or the Pharisees believed in him?"

Meditations & Lessons

✦   It seems clear that the Pharisees saw themselves as above the law rather than subject to it. They were not so much servant-interpreters of the Scripture but more manipulators of its meaning. In practice, of course, this is difficult to determine because of the way arguments can be used to defend a position. But it is a constant danger for the Church as well. Sincere, open-minded prayer is essential.

✦   The Pharisees expected that those who worked for them should believe everything they said. Surely loyalty and obedience can be expected, but we cannot presume that the salary we pay also buys the mind and will of that person. That is slavery of the most complete kind. However, this presumption is often made in real life.

JOHN 7:50-51

Nicodemus...said to them, "Does our law condemn a person before it first hears him and finds out what he is doing?"

MEDITATIONS & LESSONS

✦ The law is one thing; the words and actions of the accused are another, and there are always two sides to every story. The accusers knew the law, so they framed their reporting to indicate that Jesus was violating the law. Even if the accuser is sincere and truthful in his own mind, his choice of words can greatly prejudice a case. The accused always deserves his day in court. The very same facts may take on an entirely different appearance when reported from a different viewpoint with slightly different words.

JOHN 7:52

They answered and said to him, "You are not from Galilee also, are you?"

MEDITATIONS & LESSONS

✦ The prejudice is evident. Nothing good can come from Galilee. Only the crowd made up of inferior people could possibly defend Jesus and then, only because he is one of them. The rhetorical question is an "off the cuff" remark, but at the same time it reveals an elitist prejudice. We may say that we are interested in the facts, but if our minds are filled with prejudice, the facts can easily be distorted.

John 8:4-5

"Teacher, this woman was caught in the very act of committing adultery. Now in the law, Moses commanded us to stone such women. So what do you say?"

Meditations & Lessons

   ✦   What Jesus said about her was "I do not condemn you," but he added, "Go and sin no more." For us, this story, evokes the centuries-old Christian axiom that we should hate the sin but love the sinner. There is always hope for conversion. And even when the person does not repent, what good does condemnation do for the accuser? But forgiveness always brings its own reward.

   ✦   Jesus makes clear in the Gospels that it would be scandalous to reveal the private life of anyone. In our own day, when the media reveals the public life of most people, they become disqualified for positions of trust. Perhaps the greatest sign of Christ's divinity is that no one could "convict him of sin".

   ✦   Sexual sins have always been looked upon as among the most serious. Responsibility is often lessened by passion, but sexual sins are still very serious because of the threat they bring to the very fabric of society. They destroy the sense of fidelity, trust, privacy, and security which is necessary to a peaceful society.

John 8:18-19

"I testify on my behalf and so does the Father who sent me." So they said to him, "Where is your father?"

MEDITATIONS & LESSONS

✦   In using the terms "father" and "son" to explain his relationship to God, Jesus may be presenting a concept to the Pharisees that was truly difficult for them to fathom. On the other hand, regardless of the precise meaning that his words might have had, surely they would understand that he was claiming a very close and unusual relationship to God. This, together with his other words and deeds, should have forced the Pharisees to study his claims more closely instead of coming to the immediate conclusion that he was guilty of blasphemy and should be put to death.

John 8:21-22

He said to them again, "I am going away and you will look for me, but you will die in your sin. Where I am going you cannot come." So the Jews said, "He is not going to kill himself, is he, because he said, 'Where I am going you cannot come?'"

MEDITATIONS & LESSONS

✦   This question is astounding. The Jews look upon themselves as those who keep the Commandments—holy people—and therefore, the only "place" they cannot go is into sin. Their pride and self-righteousness is evident. After all they have seen, they still think that they are holier than Jesus, when no one could convict him of sin.

John 8:25

So they said to him, "Who are you?"

Meditations & Lessons

+   They finally ask a question which can lead them to faith, and, in fact "many came to believe in him (verse 30)." In many ways, Jesus' answer—"When you lift up the Son of Man, then you will realize that I AM"—must have seemed mysterious and mystical to those who heard him, and it rings with truth and authority.

John 8:31-33

Jesus then said to those Jews who believed in him, "If you remain in my word, you will truly be my disciples, and you will know the truth, and the truth will set you free." They answered him, "We are descendants of Abraham and have never been enslaved to anyone. How can you say, 'You will become free'?"

Meditations & Lessons

+   Jesus speaks of freedom in a spiritual sense, "Everyone who commits sin is a slave of sin (verse 34)." He knew that we are all sinners. Perfect freedom is to be in complete conformity with the will of God. In that state, there can be no sin.

+   The Jews, of course, had been in bondage several times. They probably meant that they have never willingly surrendered and never gave up their faith in God. Indeed, if they examined Christ's words in the light of that experience, they might have understood his point.

✦ Freedom is a gift of God, by which we are able to choose between his will and our own. When we choose his truth, we enjoy the fruits of freedom—peace, joy, and charity. When we choose another way, we find ourselves further and further away from the fruits of freedom, that is, further away from God, who is charity, joy, and peace.

John 8:46-48

"If I am telling the truth, why do you not believe me? Whoever belongs to God hears the words of God; for this reason you do not listen, because you do not belong to God." The Jews answered and said to him, "Are we not right in saying that you are a Samaritan and are possessed?"

Meditations & Lessons

✦ Jesus does not respond to the people's taunts with anger. Instead he gives further testimony of his divine origin—"I am not possessed. I honor my Father, but you dishonor me. I do not seek my own glory; there is one who seeks it and he is the one who judges (verses 49-50)." Indeed, if they seriously believed that he might be possessed by a demon, they would at least be admitting that he had super-human power. Then the question would be the source of his power. Jesus could easily answer by pointing out that Satan is not responsible for good works. The contention that Jesus was possessed by a demon could hardly have been a serious.

John 8:53

"Are you greater than our father Abraham, who died? Or the prophets, who died? Who do you make yourself out to be?"

Meditations & Lessons

✦　Jesus' calm answers reveal ever more clearly his claim to divinity. But his adversaries still refuse to examine that claim. They act as if they believe the promised Messiah will not be greater than Abraham. That hardly makes sense.

✦　It seems more difficult for human beings to accept and believe in God's goodness rather than to accept hardship and suffering from his hands. This may be a tacit acknowledgment of sinfulness—a belief that we deserve to be punished and are unworthy of God's favor. In a way, rejecting Christ is refusing to believe that God can be so good to me that he sends the Messiah. Although healings of the present day may be a passing phenomenon, anyone who utterly rejects them is thinking like the Jews. To suspend judgment or to accept them is at least to admit that God can be and is good to man.

John 8:56-57

"Abraham your father rejoiced to see my day; he saw it and was glad." So the Jews said to him, "You are not yet fifty years old and you have seen Abraham?"

Meditations & Lessons

✦　God-made-man was apparently too much for the Jews to believe. Were it not for their misconceptions, they surely would have understood that the Messiah was to be greater than Abraham and greater than they could have conceived. The man who stood before them—shorter than some in the crowd, heavier than others, etc.— could not possibly be the Messiah! It was indeed their prejudice that prevented them from being open to the reality of who Jesus was. Would we be in the same position? What of the resistance to apparitions at Lourdes and elsewhere, to healings, and to other manifestations of God's presence and grace?

John 9:2

His disciples asked him, "Rabbi, who sinned, this man or his parents, that he was born blind?"

Meditations & Lessons

+ Today, physical handicaps and material setbacks may not seem as the consequence of sin, but they are still perceived as mistakes (someone's fault), accidents or bad luck—as if they are the result of something evil or harmful. We have a tendency to blame the victim.

+ Handicapped people can make a great contribution to the welfare of others, especially their spiritual welfare. They can inspire multitudes to compassion and to acts of charity, who otherwise might never be touched.

+ There is a saying that God brings good out of everything, even misfortunes. There is no question about the truth of this statement. However, if we have a pessimistic outlook, we shall never find the good. But if we allow ourselves to look for the good, we shall surely find it.

John 9:6-10

He spat on the ground and made clay with the saliva, and smeared the clay on his eyes, and said to him, "Go wash in the Pool of Siloam" (which means Sent). So he went and washed, and came back able to see...So they said to him, "[So] how were your eyes opened?"

MEDITATIONS & LESSONS

✦   The blind man's neighbors might have been ready to accept some amazing explanation, even an accidental healing, but they were hardly ready to accept mud and water as a means of regaining sight. The miracle was an invitation to look beyond the method of healing to the Person who had been instrumental in the man regaining his eyesight.

JOHN 9:12

And they said to him, "Where is he?"

MEDITATIONS & LESSONS

✦   They ask the right question; they seek the person who performed the miracle. However, the whole context leads to questions about their motivation. It seems that they are automatically going to put him on trial as Beelzebub, rather than consider what relationship he must have with God.

JOHN 9:13-16

They brought the one who was once blind to the Pharisees. Now Jesus had made clay and opened his eyes on a sabbath...So some of the Pharisees said, "This man is not from God because he does not keep the sabbath." [But] others said, "How can a sinful man do such signs?"

MEDITATIONS & LESSONS

✦ Finally the Pharisees asked the right question. Indeed, how could a sinner work the miracles that Jesus worked? Here is the possiblity that some Pharisees were able to see the truth.

✦ Good and evil are in direct opposition. Some of those who witnessed Jesus' actions instinctively realized this. They knew that healing comes from God and that a sinner, or an evil man, would not have his power. But others were so blind or their hearts were so hardened that they could not see the truth. To them, it was more important that Jesus seemed to break the rule (healing on the sabbath) than that he was working miraculous cures.

✦ Even today, we see the same reaction. People find excuses for not believing in Jesus. Often, it is because someone who professes to follow Jesus does not.

✦ There are times that we only see what is obvious through the grace of God. We know that Jesus healed the blind. Therefore, we know that he is the Son of God. There are many, however, who do not see with the eyes of faith.

JOHN 9:17

So they said to the blind man again, "What do you have to say about him, since he opened your eyes?"

MEDITATIONS & LESSONS

✦ There is no question in the mind of the blind man that only the power of God could have cured him. So regardless of who Jesus is precisely, he is certainly of God.

+   It is strange that the Pharisees even asked the question, except that there was some degree of disagreement among them. So the grace of conversion was given to them. But as the rest of the questioning reveals, their prejudice was too deep to be changed.

John 9:18-19

Now the Jews did not believe that he had been blind and gained his sight until they summoned the parents of the one who had gained his sight. They asked them, "Is this your son, who you say was born blind? How does he now see?"

Meditations & Lessons

+   The parents of the blind man attest to the fact that he was born blind. However, they refuse to say how it is that he can now see. John tells us that they were afraid that if they acknowledged Jesus they would be expelled from the synagogue. For some it is very difficult to acknowledge the truth of God's action in their lives.

+   The leaders of the people work through fear and manipulation to deny that Jesus is Messiah. These are evil tools. Jesus works through love to demonstrate that he has been sent by the Father.

John 9:24-26

So a second time they called the man who had been blind and said to him, "Give God the praise! We know that this man is a sinner." He replied, "If he is a sinner, I do not know. One thing I do know is that I was blind and now I see." So they said to him, "What did he do to you? How did he open your eyes?"

MEDITATIONS & LESSONS

✦ The Pharisees refuse to see the obvious. They are frantically looking for someway to deny the reality of Christ's power and goodness. They will go to any lengths to deny the truth.

JOHN 9:27

He answered them, "I told you already, and you did not listen. Why do you want to hear it again? Do you want to become his disciples too?"

MEDITATIONS & LESSONS

✦ Either the blind man is ingenuous or he has been emboldened by his faith in Jesus. In any case, he stands on the facts. He was blind and now he sees. Nothing the Pharisees say can overcome this reality.

JOHN 9:28-34

They ridiculed him and said, "You are that man's disciples; we are disciples of Moses! We know that God spoke to Moses, but we do not know where this one is from." The man answered and said to them, "This is what is so amazing, that you do not know where he is from, yet he opened my eyes. We know that God does not listen to sinners, but if one is devout and does his will, he listens to him. It is unheard of that anyone ever opened the eyes of a person born blind. If this man were not from God, he would not be able to do anything." They answered and said to him, "You were born totally in sin, and are you trying to teach us?"

Meditations & Lessons

✦   It was a common belief among the Jews that physical evil was due to sin. Since there was confusion about the immortality of the soul, a just God would be required to settle problems on earth in a just manner. He would require an eye for an eye and a tooth for a tooth, as it were. Riches were taken as a sign of great virtue.

✦   The Pharisees were among the relatively small educated class. How could they learn anything from anyone else? Of course, the world is full of examples of bright people having no common sense, or those in power making decisions in light of what is for their own immediate good, only to find that the decisions are immediately tragic for some, and in the long run tragic for themselves.

✦   The blind man displays the courage of one who truly believes. The Pharisees display the blindness of the smug and self-satisfied. They are the elite. They are so great that they can deny the facts.

John 9:35-36

When Jesus heard that they [the Pharisees] had thrown him [the blind man] out [of the synagogue], he found him and said to him, "Do you believe in the Son of Man?" He answered and said, "Who is he, sir, that I may believe in him?"

Meditations & Lessons

✦   The blind man was so convinced of his cure—and well he might be—that he was ready to accept anything that his healer would say, because he believed that Christ had power from God. We claim to believe that Christ is the very Son of God and yet our faith is so weak and many other "believers" refuse to accept and follow his teachings!

JOHN 9:39-40

Then Jesus said, "I came into this world for judgment, so that those who do not see might see, and those who do see might become blind." Some of the Pharisees who were with him heard this and said to him, "Surely, we are not also blind, are we?"

MEDITATIONS & LESSONS

✦ The Pharisees are not blind physically, and they should not be blind spiritually due to their education and background. However, they have deliberately blindfolded themselves with prejudice. The blind man believes; those who should be able to see Christ's identity most clearly, disbelieve.

JOHN 10:17-20

"This is why the Father loves me, because I lay down my life in order to take it up again. No one takes it from me, but I lay it down on my own. I have power to lay it down, and power to take it up again. This command I have received from my Father." Again there was division among the Jews because of these words. Many of them said, "He is possessed and out of his mind; why listen to him?"

Meditations & Lessons

✦   Rather than say, "Let's listen to more and then decide whether Christ is a demon or of God," the Jews reversed the sequence. They were not ready to listen. They had made their decision on emotional and/or other grounds before all the evidence could be given.

✦   The Jews hardness of heart, stiff-necked, blind attitude prevented them from looking at Jesus with open minds.

John 10:19-21

Again there was division among the Jews because of these words. Many of them said, "He is possessed and out of his mind, why listen to him? Others said, "These are not the words of one possessed; surely a demon cannot open the eyes of the blind, can he?"

Meditations & Lessons

✦   There were some who were willing to look at the facts. So the majority must have experienced some discomfort when some of their own people were willing at least to discuss the source of Jesus' power. But they were too stubborn or too proud or too blind to listen.

John 10:22-24

It was winter. And Jesus walked about in the temple area on the Portico of Solomon. So the Jews gathered around him and said to him, "How long are you going to keep us in suspense?"

MEDITATIONS & LESSONS

✦ The Lord does not keep us in suspense with regard to his divinity. It is our own doubts and disbelief that bring about our anxiety. The Lord explains himself as clearly as he can, but there is always room for doubt, because the human mind cannot fully comprehend the infinite. It takes faith to accept God, and although the evidence can make the act of faith reasonable, the evidence will never logically force a particular conclusion.

JOHN 11:8

The disciples said to him, "Rabbi, the Jews were just trying to stone you, and you want to go back there?"

MEDITATIONS & LESSONS

✦ Jesus' response is that we have nothing whatsoever to fear, if truth is on our side. The only thing that others can do is to put us to death, which in fact is a great gift. We all fear death to a greater or lesser extent, but that fear diminishes in proportion to our faith in God, our trust in his truth and in his promises.

JOHN 11:35-37

And Jesus wept. So the Jews said, "See how he loved him." But some of them said, "Could not the one who opened the eyes of the blind man have done something so that this man would not have died?"

MEDITATIONS & LESSONS

✦   Dying is looked upon as a great evil. Is it bad to die? To go to God? To "Abraham's bosom"? It would seem so both to the Jews and to ourselves, but if so, our faith is not as deep as it can be.

✦   The Lord allowed Lazarus to die in order to show his power over life and death. This question implies that the Jews would believe his claims to divinity, if he could bring Lazarus back from the dead (or prevent his death) and yet they did not believe. Faith is a gift of God, always extended but not always accepted. A skeptical attitude is a great obstacle.

JOHN 11:46-47

Some of them went to the Pharisees and told them what Jesus had done. So the chief priests and the Pharisees convened the Sanhedrin and said, "What are we going to do?"

MEDITATIONS & LESSONS

✦   They finally admit that Christ has given them many signs and that many people are beginning to believe, but instead of rejoicing that the Messiah is in their midst, they are fearful that his presence will have political repercussions.

✦   So now, the foes of Jesus were reduced to thinking about how they could save their own skins. They were willing to sacrifice the hope of Israel to protect themselves.

JOHN 11:56

They looked for Jesus and said to one another as they were in the temple area, "What do you think? That he will not come to the feast?"

Meditations & Lessons

✦ John gives the impression that the precarious situation of Jesus was an open secret. Everyone seemed to be aware of the attitude of the Pharisees. Many had opinions in the matter that differed from the Pharisees. We are told that "many came to believe", but they were merely playing the role of bystanders, and they were not about to open their mouths. They knew how the man-born-blind had been treated, and they were not about to expose themselves to ridicule or danger.

✦ It is pretty obvious that those asking the question knew that it was inadvisable to come to the feast. They would not have come in his place. They anticipate that if he does come it will be sensational, especially if he wins. If he loses, there will be a crucifixion.

✦ There were two things that seemed inconceivable. First, they could not believe that Jesus who had always bested the Pharisees could possibly be defeated by them. Secondly, they did not see that his fate had anything to do with their personal lives. They did not appreciate (or maybe they did and would not face it) that Jesus was looking for acceptance from the ordinary person more than from the Pharisees. The Pharisees thought they had much to lose if Jesus were the Messiah. The people had everything to gain. Yet, they took no action to support Jesus.

JOHN 12:4-5

Then Judas the Iscariot, one [of] his disciples, and the one who would betray him, said, "Why was this oil not sold for three hundred days' wages and given to the poor?"

Meditations & Lessons

✦   There is no shame in giving generously of what we have to the worship of God. The greatest gift that we can give to anyone is faith in God, whether the person is rich or poor.

✦   Is money the only consideration in the world? Are there no other values? What if a man gains the whole world and suffers the loss of his soul? Jesus came not to give money to the materially poor, but to give his very life for the spiritually poor, that is, all of us.

John 12:31-34

"Now is the time of judgment on this world; now the ruler of this world will be driven out. And when I am lifted up from the earth, I will draw everyone to myself." He said this indicating the kind of death he would die. So the crowd answered him, "We have heard from the law that the Messiah remains forever. Then how can you say that the Son of Man must be lifted up? Who is this Son of Man?"

Meditations & Lessons

✦   This does seem to be a puzzling phrase, especially in light of the fact that many did not believe in the immortality of the soul and most had not believed in the signs that Christ had performed. Christ seems at this point to be musing to himself or to be going on the record so that after the Resurrection the meaning of his words would become clear.

JOHN 13:5-6

Then he poured water into a basin and began to wash the disciples' feet and to dry them with the towel around his waist. He came to Simon Peter, who said to him, "Master, are you going to wash my feet?"

MEDITATIONS & LESSON

✦ Peter was scandalized. The Master was doing the work of a slave or a servant. Although Jesus did not lord it over his Apostles, his superiority was evident to them. He was far superior to any worldly master because he had no need of material support. There was a supernatural aura about him. And yet, here he was washing the feet of the Disciples!

✦ Peter had a degree of pride in himself, of course, but he also knew his humble origins. In his circles there were no slaves who washed his feet. As a fisherman, he simply did not travel in that company. So his surprise was not only in the gesture of Christ, but that he would wash the feet of an ordinary fisherman.

JOHN 13:25

He [John] leaned back against Jesus' chest and said to him, "Master, who is it?"

MEDITATIONS & LESSONS

✦ Jesus had just told the Apostles that one of them would betray him. The Apostles certainly had at least the normal human curiosity that we manifest today about "news," scandals, and the like. And once we get the information, what do we do with it? In this case it seems that the answer could not have been as clear as the account seems to indicate; it seems sure that all of the Apostles would have acted to restrain Judas.

JOHN 13:33-36

"My children, I will be with you only a little while longer. You will look for me, and as I told the Jews, 'Where I go you cannot come,' so now I say it to you.".....Simon Peter said to him, "Master, where are you going?"

MEDITATIONS & LESSONS

✦   Jesus may be speaking of death or heaven or both. It doesn't matter. There is an appointed time for everyone. In the case of Christ, however, the ultimate destination was clear; not so with ourselves. Our day to day direction needs to be the same as his—the Father's will. Given that, there is no concern about our ultimate destination.

JOHN 13:37

Peter said to him, "Master, why can't I follow you now?"

MEDITATIONS & LESSONS

✦   After the fact, these questions would seem rather foolish, but not beforehand. Peter rightly believed that Jesus had the power to do anything. He did not seem to understand that Jesus would not be doing everything for him forever. Jesus wants to aid us, to work in and through us, but something is required of us as well. We must place our will in conformity with the Lord's; we must resist temptation to selfishness and evil; we must positively choose to be one with Christ and not just drift along with him, depending on our own wishful thinking and his salvific will to work wonders.

JOHN 14:5

Thomas said to him, "Master, we do not know where you are going; how can we know the way?"

MEDITATIONS & LESSONS

✦   Thomas is right. We have to know where we are going in order to get there. Heaven is an exception. We do not know where it is, nor can we find it by ourselves. But that does not matter. Jesus is the Way, and if we imitate him to the best of our ability, we will get there.

✦   Faith is required. But we have seen the way; we know it well; we cannot lose the way unless we deliberately wander from it; and if we humbly admit that we have lost the way at anytime, no matter how far we have wandered, the Lord will put us back on track.

JOHN 14:19-22

"In a little while the world will no longer see me, but you will see me, because I live and you will live. On that day you will realize that I am in my Father and you are in me and I in you. Whoever has my commandments and observes them is the one who loves me. And whoever loves me will be loved by my Father, and I will love him and reveal myself to him." Judas, not the

Iscariot, said to him, "Master, [then] what happened that you will reveal yourself to us and not to the world?"

MEDITATIONS & LESSONS

✦   Jesus is speaking about an intimate association. Every person is given the opportunity to know Jesus, but he manifests himself in this intimate sense—makes himself one—only with those who believe in him.

✦   The way in which Jesus juxtaposes "the world" and "us" seems to indicate that the number of true believers will always be a minority, "a remnant." Those who choose to love the world and trust in it will be more numerous than the believers—those who put their faith in God, his promises, "the higher realm."

JOHN 16:17-18

So some of his disciples said to one another, "What does this mean that he is saying to us, 'A little while and you will not see me, and again a little while and you will see me,' and 'Because I am going to the Father'?" So they said "What is this 'little while' [of which he speaks]? We do not know what he means."

MEDITATIONS & LESSONS

✦   Jesus is referring to a great mystery—his death and resurrection, and perhaps his ascension. He may, too, be referring to the death of his Disciples. They could not possibly understand what he was saying until they experienced it. The important point is that he has power over death. As he says in the last verse, "I have overcome the world" (John 16:33).

✦ The words of Jesus indicate that the Disciples also will overcome the world in some sense and that there is life after death—a life in which we shall be joined to the Lord.

✦ Time is quite relative. All time is short except eternity. It may not seem so as we are enduring some pain, but all things in this world are passing, and passing rather quickly at that.

JOHN 18:17

Then the maid who was the gatekeeper said to Peter, "You are not one of this man's disciples, are you?"

MEDITATIONS & LESSONS

✦ Peter's denial was probably made in John's presence. He reacted out of fear, and so he lied. And yet after Pentecost, he consistently told the truth, preached the Gospel, regardless of the danger to his life. At the time Peter denied Jesus, he had not yet received the promised gift of the Holy Spirit.

✦ What it comes down to is that at this point Jesus was still recognized as a man only. It is difficult to die for a good man. Here, the Lord was in disgrace. He seemed weak and powerless. The righteous were against him and had him in their power. "Lack of divinity" made the difference as faith in divinity would make the difference later.

JOHN 18:22

When he had said this, one of temple guards standing there struck Jesus and said, "Is this the way you answer the high priest?"

Meditations & Lessons

✦   The Pharisees were apparently looking at first for a compromise agreement in secret. Jesus, like St. Paul later, appealed for a full hearing with witnesses. To a great extent Church "trials" have been conducted secretly; perhaps it would be a good idea to make them more public. The truth would definitely be on the side of Church authority in disputes of late, but the communications media might greatly distort the entire debate. Still, the matter needs thought.

✦   The response of the Lord was not disrespectful; he was simply asking the high priest to carry out his avowed duties properly. The officer's reaction is a good indication of the manner in which we sometimes act. We take the part of one person or another, whom we like or trust, without considering the facts of the matter as carefully as we might. Even the high priest should be held to truth and justice.

John 18:25

Now Simon Peter was standing there keeping warm. And they said to him, "You are not one of his disciples are you?"

Meditations & Lessons

✦   Once committed to a lie, it is difficult to withdraw. As the evidence became even stronger against Peter, he became all the more insistent in his denials. Human nature is frail indeed; the power of God's grace immense. When he placed trust in his own strength, he failed miserably. In his preaching thereafter, Peter was free in confessing his guilt, and, strengthened by God's grace, he died for Christ.

John 18:26

One of the slaves of the high priest, a relative of the one whose ear Peter had cut off, said, "Didn't I see you in the garden with him?"

Meditations & Lessons

✦ There is a significance to the fact that Peter denied Jesus three times. One denial could have been almost overlooked. Peter could have claimed as we do, "I didn't have time to think," or "I didn't know what I was saying." Even a second denial may have been explained as caused by the stress of the moment or uttered without sufficient thought. But the third denial, made it clear to Peter that he had in fact denied his Lord. His denials, which Jesus had predicted, became important to Peter and to us. We learn that the Lord will forgive us and that it is possible for us to change.

✦ As a matter of fact, Peter probably had very little to fear from the servants. He was more or less one of them, so there probably was not much danger of his being reported and arrested. The man who saw him in the garden would realize that the soldiers had released the Disciples.

John 18:29

So Pilate came out to them and said, "What charge do you bring [against] this man?"

Meditations & Lessons

✦ Pilate initiated the trial in a legal manner, but it was clear from the Jewish response that they had no intention of allowing mere legalities to interfere with what they had already decided. It was only after Pilate's insistence on legality that they went through the motions, accused Christ of sedition, and had Pilate pronounce a sentence of death, even though the charges had in no way been proven.

JOHN 18:33

Pilate went back into the praetorium and summoned Jesus and said to him, "Are you the King of the Jews?"

MEDITATIONS & LESSONS

✦ In answering Pilate—"Do you say this on your own or have others told you about me (verse 34)?"—Jesus invited him to discuss his identity. Pilate had obviously heard reports about Jesus, but he probably asked the question out of personal interest or, at least, curiosity.

JOHN 18:35

Pilate answered, "I am not a Jew, am I? Your own nation and the chief priests handed you over to me. What have you done?"

MEDITATIONS & LESSONS

✦ For some reason, Pilate denied his interest in Jesus. Perhaps he was embarrassed that people could think he was interested in Jewish law or issues. He seemed to indicate that he had no interest in Jesus or whether he was king of the Jews.

✦ Jesus had done nothing that could warrant his arrest. His offense was preaching the truth and announcing to the world the source of that truth. And because both of these realities were difficult to accept and impossible to refute, he was put to death. It still works this way. In one way or another we silence or get rid of those whom we cannot seem to control.

JOHN 18:36-37

Jesus answered, "My kingdom does not belong to this world. If my kingdom did belong to this world, my attendants would be fighting to keep me from being handed over to the Jews. But as it is, my kingdom is not here." So Pilate said to him, "Then you are a king?"

MEDITATIONS & LESSONS

✦   Jesus' response indicates that he is more than a mere earthly king.

✦   Communication is a difficult art. Jesus did well, of course, but much depends upon the hearers. Hearing, the Pharisees did not hear; seeing, the Pharisees did not see.

JOHN 18:37-38

Jesus answered, "You say I am a king. For this I was born and for this I came into the world, to testify to the truth. Everyone who belongs to the truth listens to my voice." Pilate said to him, "What is truth?"

MEDITATIONS & LESSONS

✦   The question is difficult to interpret. But it seems to connote contempt for truth. Pilate may be saying that there is no such thing as truth, or that it is impossible to know truth, or that the truth is of no consequence and has no power, or that truth is something that is determined arbitrarily.

✦   To Pilate, someone who testified to the truth could seem to be a fool. Perhaps, Pilate thought that there is no future in fighting for truth because it is so easy to overcome. Things are not much different today. Objective truth is being ignored in every area in favor of subjective, self-centered opinion. And yet, even as this happens, it is evident that truth will survive or the world will go mad.

✦   Pilate apparently did not wait for Jesus to answer his question. Many people do not wait to hear what truth is about.

JOHN 18:38-39

When he had said this, he again went out to the Jews and said to them, "I find no guilt in him. But you have a custom that I release one prisoner to you at Passover. Do you want me to release to you the King of the Jews?"

MEDITATIONS & LESSONS

✦   To Pilate, because Jesus' only weapon was the truth, or the use of words, Jesus seemed helpless and harmless. So Pilate could not believe that the Jews were as opposed to him as they seemed to be. But by asking the Jews to make a decision, Pilate was abdicating his responsibility. Once Pilate started down that road, there was no turning back. Now the people were the judges, and Pilate the advocate pleading with them for the life of Jesus.

✦   Pilate's use of the word "king" stirred up the scribes and Pharisees. It is amazing that human beings so frequently choose evil over good for emotional reasons. The only "harm" that Jesus could do was predicated on truth. If he spoke the truth, the whole nation might go over to him, Barabbas, evil though he was, could never have accomplished this.

JOHN 19:7-9

The Jews answered, "We have a law, and according to that law he ought to die, because he made himself the Son of God." Now when Pilate heard this statement, he became even more afraid, and went back into the praetorium and said to Jesus, "Where are you from?"

MEDITATIONS & LESSONS

✦ Christ allowed the charge—that he claimed to be the Son of God—to stand. Pilate was incredulous, but because of his superstitious outlook, he took the charge seriously, but at the same time there was not a chance that Pilate could be convinced of Christ's divinity. The charge only raised the level of Pilate's anxiety. He could not have released Jesus, even though he may have wanted to. He was on the defensive.

✦ Without faith, we like Pilate, take the course we fear least.

JOHN 19:10

So Pilate said to him, "Do you not speak to me? Do you not know that I have power to release you and I have power to crucify you?"

MEDITATIONS & LESSONS

✦ Pilate had the civil power to crucify Christ, but not the moral power over an innocent person. He knew both and was worried. No one has power over the just and innocent. Once again, Christ's answer was perfect to spark a conversion in Pilate, but he still could not give fair consideration to Christ's offer.

✦   Perhaps a truly wicked person would not realize that there is a power higher than himself, but by and large, heavy responsibility leads to humility. I had wondered why I found this to be so in the personages whom I met in Rome; now I know. If someone is in a position of power and lacks humility, he has lost a sense of who he is, and to that degree he has probably misplaced God in his life as well as himself.

JOHN 19:14-15

It was preparation day for Passover, and it was about noon. And he said to the Jews, "Behold, your king!" They cried out, "Take him away, take him away! Crucify him!" Pilate said to them, "Shall I crucify your king?"

MEDITATIONS & LESSONS

✦   Christ had now become a play-thing for Pilate. Pilate's use of the word "king" was dripping with irony and surely must have further incensed the Jews.

✦   This was a cat and mouse game for Pilate and the Jews. The question was no longer about who Jesus was, it was about who would win the cat and mouse game. Priests can find themselves in that kind of political maneuvering—so priests should never meddle in politics. For example, we know where we stand on pro-life. But some can embrace questionable methods and try to use clergy in order to support their methods and actions.

✦   Neither Pilate nor the Jews were prepared to accept Christ as their king. Are we? Do we sometimes reject him, when the going gets tough. Most every temptation is such a case, and sin is a rejection. The crowd is against his teaching, so we are tempted to put him aside and to do what is more convenient, more suited to our personal interest.

John 20:11-13

But Mary stayed outside the tomb weeping. And as she wept, she bent over into the tomb and saw two angels in white sitting there, one at the head and one at the feet where the body of Jesus had been. And they said to her, "Woman, why are you weeping?"

Meditations & Lessons

✦ For those who have faith, weeping is inappropriate at the time of death. We may weep anyway due to human circumstances, but the beginning of a new, glorious, eternal life is hardly an occasion for tears. Funerals of religious are always inspiring due to the lack of tears and the note of hope that faith produces. These funerals are always occasions of joy, manifestations of faith, hope and love.

✦ Surely our tears should not be for the deceased. We trust that God in his mercy will reward the person. In any event, we can do nothing to change their situation. If there are tears, they are shed for ourselves, as Mary's were, because we have lost someone, who was good to us and whom we should have appreciated more in life. When this gets through to us, however—that the tears are for ourselves—they should quickly dry.

John 21:21

When Peter saw him [John], he said, "Lord, what about him?"

Meditations & Lessons

✦   Jesus' answer—"What concern is it of yours? You follow me."—is meant for all of us. In other words, we should keep our eyes on Jesus and not on each other.

✦   Each of us has a unique, personal relationship with God. It may seem that God loves others more than us, or that he is not treating us fairly. Yet we can be certain that what happens in our life is for our good. God gives us opportunities for virtue, not stumbling blocks, which lead to vice. On the other hand, we do need strength of will to perform the virtuous act and "merit" a reward.

✦   Envy of others is of no profit to ourselves. Each of us has enough to do in dealing with ourselves, without worrying about the other person. Let the Lord be concerned, as he surely is.

✦   Seeming to have favorites can be disturbing to others. In fact, the "favorite" often has greater burdens to carry, but not in the eyes of the others. Leaders should strive not to give the impression that there are favorites. Others can feel rejected—and the leader has an obligation to be helpful to all.